Readings in Literary Criticism III
CRITICS ON POPE

CRITICS ON POPE

Readings in Literary Criticism

Edited by Judith O'Neill

London GEORGE ALLEN & UNWIN
Boston   Sydney

First published 1968

Third impression 1978

GEORGE ALLEN & UNWIN LTD
40 Museum Street, London WC1A 1LU

This anthology © George Allen & Unwin Ltd, 1968

ISBN 0 04 801006 5

821.5 cri
POP
O'N

Printed in Great Britain
by Billing & Sons Ltd, Guildford, London and Worcester

INTRODUCTION

The first part of this book traces, in a series of short extracts, the changes in taste and critical judgment that have affected Pope's reputation as a poet over two centuries. In his own lifetime he was praised and idolized by his friends and by the literary world in general. At the same time he was scorned and attacked by his enemies (John Dennis, for example) with an extraordinary force of personal spite and venom. Both friends and enemies were as concerned to defend or attack his morals and his character as to assess the poems themselves. Joseph Warton, writing in 1756, was one of the first to distinguish between those poems he thought would last (*Windsor Forest, The Rape of the Lock, Eloisa to Abelard*), and the later satires which he felt to be merely transitory. Most critics on Pope today would completely reverse this judgment and would value *The Dunciad, Arbuthnot* and the *Moral Essays* much higher than the earlier 'tender' pieces.

Amongst the Romantic critics, Pope was regarded with suspicion and condescension rather than the outright hostility that is often attributed to them. They damned him with faint praise and spoke in patronizing terms of his technical skill, but they hardly regarded him as a real poet. A sharp pamphlet war broke out between W. L. Bowles on the one side and Lord Byron and Thomas Campbell on the other. Bowles was an editor of Pope's works who deplored his ignorance of Nature—in the sense of mountains, trees and flowers. Byron's arguments in defence of Pope are often flamboyant and outrageous but he emerges as a man with an unusually sensitive appreciation of Pope's imaginative power.

The Victorians were even less responsive to Pope than most of the Romantics had been. Arnold gave his famous dictum in 1880—Pope and Dryden 'are not classics of our poetry, they are classics of our prose'. This became the general opinion for the next forty years. The steady swing away from Pope in the public taste had gone as far as it could go.

The first sign of a drastic revaluation came in 1922 with the brief but perceptive comment by John Middleton Murry, and in the same year Eliot's praise of Dryden helped to re-instate the whole Augustan period. William Empson's illuminating comment on the 'laughing Ceres' lines of Moral Essay IV and Edith Sitwell's extravagently sympathetic biography, both in 1930, were followed by a detailed exploration of particular poems in F. R. Leavis's classic essay of 1933. We regret that we were not given permission to reprint an extract from this important article. A few years later came Geoffrey Tillotson's scholarly full-length study, *On the Poetry of Pope*, and G. Wilson Knight's long essay, *The Vital Flame*. By 1939 Pope's reputation as a poet had begun to recover from its long, slow decline and, as the revolution in taste gathered strength, general readers of his poems became aware, for the first time, of the particular kind of pleasure he could give and aware too of his rich and tragi-comic view of man and the world.

In the second part of the book, 'Critics on Pope since 1940', I have had three aims in mind. I wanted, first, to give the student a collection of essays that would help him to enjoy and understand a good range of Pope's poetry and so I have tried to include something on each of the major poems, or at least on each kind of poem. I have had to leave out several interesting essays (Cleanth Brooks on the *Rape of the Lock*, for example) because I could not include too much discussion of any one poem at the expense of others. Then I have tried to give something from each of the more distinguished names in recent Pope criticism—George Sherburn, for example, Maynard Mack, Edward Niles Hooker, Ian Jack, R. A. Brower—as well as work from some lesser known but often equally perceptive critics. I have preferred Mack's essay, *The Muse of Satire*, to his better known, *Wit and Poetry and Pope: Some Observations on his Imagery*, because it is less familiar and less accessible to most students.

My third aim has been to give some idea of the different *kinds* of recent criticism on Pope, encouraging the student to approach the poems in several quite different ways. The essays by J. M. Cameron and E. N. Hooker, for example, explore two key ideas in Pope's work— 'nature' and 'wit'. These essays draw on only one poem, but they raise questions that are basic to the study of all Pope's poetry. Cameron writes as a philosopher, tracing the history of an idea and its various meanings for Pope. Hooker writes more as an historian, gathering extracts from contemporary sermons and pamphlets to illuminate the intellectual climate in which Pope was writing. Thomas R. Edwards and Elias F. Mengel on the other hand, examine in detail the pattern of imagery and meaning in two poems and R. A. Brower's concern is with the enriching and subtle allusions that Pope makes to those ancient classical writers so familiar to his first readers but often completely unknown to the reader today. S. L. Goldberg's essay is quite different again. He looks at Pope's work as a whole and gives a masterly personal survey, making sharp and carefully argued distinctions between the less successful poems and the best. His essay is a good one to start with, and a good one to end with too, when all the other essays have been read.

Cambridge, 1968   JUDITH O'NEILL

CONTENTS

CRITICS ON POPE: 1726-1939

ALEXANDER POPE (1688-1744)

There are three distinct *tours* in poetry; the design, the language, and the versification.... After writing a poem, one should correct it all over, with one single view at a time. Thus for language; if an elegy; 'these lines are very good, but are not they of too heroical a strain?' and so *vice versa*. (1728-30)

It is a great fault, in descriptive poetry, to describe everything. (1734-6)

The things that I have written fastest, have always pleased the most. I wrote the *Essay on Criticism* fast; for I had digested all the matter, in prose, before I began upon it in verse. The *Rape of the Lock* was written fast: all the machinery was added afterwards; and the making that, and what was published before, hit so well together, is, I think, one of the greatest proofs of judgment of anything I ever did. I wrote most of the *Iliad* fast; a great deal of it on journeys, from the little pocket Homer on that shelf there; and often forty or fifty verses in a morning in bed.—The Dunciad cost me as much pains as anything I ever wrote. (1734-6)

About fifteen I got acquainted with Mr Walsh: he used to encourage me much, and used to tell me that there was one way left of excelling; for though we had several great poets, we never had any one great poet that was correct; and he desired me to make that my study and aim. (1742-3)

I am in no concern, whether people should say this is writ well or ill, but that this was writ with a good design;—'He has written in the cause of virtue, and done something to mend people's morals;' this is the only commendation I long for. (1743-4)

One must tune each line over in one's head, to try whether they go right or not.... The great rule of verse is to be musical. (1743-4)

Joseph Spence, *Anecdotes, Observations, and Characters of Books and Men, Collected from the Conversation of Mr Pope and Other Eminent Persons of His Time*, ed. S. W. Singer, 1820, newly introduced by Bonamy Dobrée, London, 1964, pp. 46, 101, 102-3, 169, 179, 184, 186.

JOSEPH SPENCE (1699-1768)

It is [Mr Pope] who took up the great rule of the *sound's being a comment on the sense* and enforced it beyond any of the critics who went before him. To this writer we chiefly owe the revival of the noble art of numbers and the method of signifying motions, and actions, and all that vast variety of our passions, by sounds.

An Essay on Mr Pope's 'Odyssey', 1726-7, 3rd ed., 1747, p. 136.

JOHN DENNIS (1657-1734)

I have always looked upon the little gentleman with whom I have to do at present ... as one absolutely without merit: for there can be no poetical merit without good sense, which he has not. ...
I look upon it to be my duty ... to pull the lion's skin from this little ass, which popular error has thrown around him, and show him in his natural shape and size ...
In all his trifles ... there is neither design nor meaning ... there is nothing like any passion finely touched nor any one character finely or truly drawn; ... the sentiments are often extravagent and absurd; the language often impure and barbarous.

Remarks Upon Mr Pope's Translation of Homer with Two Letters Concerning 'Windsor Forest' and the 'Temple of Fame', London, 1727, Preface and p. 9.

[Pope] is one whose mind was equally out of nature and equally crooked and deformed with his body. ...
[I published my earlier pamphlet on Pope's *Homer*] with a design to hold a faithful glass up to this little gentleman and to cure him of his vain and his wretched conceitedness, by giving him a view of his ignorance, his folly and his natural impotence. ...
Pope not only attacked several persons of far greater merit than himself, but like a mad Indian that runs amuck, struck out at everything that came in his way without distinction of friend or foe, acquaintance or stranger, merit or unworthiness, wisdom or folly, vice or virtue; like a blind beetle that in its blundering flight bruises itself against every object it meets and does not fail to knock itself down by the impotent blows which it gives to others. ... 'Tis to people who want understanding that he owes most of his little fortune and all his little reputation; ... he has ... no admirers among those who have capacity to discern, to distinguish and judge. ...

Thus, Sir, has this author given his fine lady Belinda in the *Rape of the Lock* beauty and good breeding, modesty and virtue in words, but in reality and in fact made her an artificial dawbing jilt, a tomrig, a virago, and a lady of the lake ... This little creature ... is as diminutive an author as he is an animal.

Remarks on Mr Pope's 'Rape of the Lock' in Several Letters to a Friend, 1728, 2nd ed. London, 1728, Dedication, Preface, and pp. 18–19, 55 (wrongly numbered 39 in this edition).

WILLIAM WARBURTON (1698-1779)

To have been one of the first poets in the world is but his second praise. He was in a higher class. He was one of the *noblest works of God*. He was an *honest man*.... His more distinguished virtues [were] his filial piety, his disinterested friendships, his reverence for the constitution of his country, his love and admiration of virtue and ... his hatred and contempt of vice, his extensive charity to the indigent, his warm benevolence to mankind, his supreme veneration of the Deity, and, above all, his sincere belief in revelation.

The Works of Alexander Pope Esq., in nine volumes with Commentaries and Notes by William Warburton, 1751, 2nd ed. Dublin, 1752, vol. I, pp. vii–viii.

JOSEPH WARTON (1722-1800)

I think one may venture to remark, that the reputation of Pope as a poet, among posterity, will be principally owing to his *Windsor Forest*, his *Rape of the Lock*, and his *Eloisa to Abelard;* whilst the facts and characters alluded to and exposed in his later writings will be forgotten and unknown, and their poignancy and propriety little relished. For wit and satire are transitory and perishable, but nature and passion are eternal....

Where then ... shall we ... place our admired Pope? Not, assuredly, in the same rank with Spenser, Shakespeare and Milton, however justly we may applaud the *Eloisa* and *Rape of the Lock*; but considering the correctness, elegance and utility of his works, the weight of sentiment, and the knowledge of man they contain, we may venture to assign him a place *next* to *Milton*, and *just* above *Dryden*.

An Essay on the Genius and Writings of Pope, vol. I, 1756; vol. II, 1782; 5th ed. London, 1806, vol. I, p. 330, vol. II, p. 404.

OWEN RUFFHEAD (1723-1769)

As to his person, it is well known that he was low in stature; and of a diminutive and mishapen figure, which no-one ridiculed more pleasantly than himself. Nevertheless, his countenance reflected the image of his mind. His eye in particular was remarkably fine, sharp and piercing: there was something in short in the air of his countenance altogether, which seemed to bespeak strong sense and acute penetration, tempered with benevolence and politeness. . . . His voice . . . was . . . naturally musical. . . . In his temper, though he was naturally mild and gentle, yet he sometimes betrayed that exquisite sensibility, which is the concomitant of genius. But though his lively perception and delicate feeling irritated by wretched ill health, made him too quickly take fire, yet his good sense and humanity soon rendered him placable. The hasty sparks of resentment presently expired; and his mind was superior to the dark malice of revenge . . . He was indeed perfectly open, unaffected and affable in his manners. He never debased himself by an unbecoming levity or servile accommodation: nor did he offend others, by an overweening arrogance and pertinacity. . . .

His heart was not, as he himself well expressed it, like a great warehouse, stored only with his own goods or with empty spaces to be supplied as fast as interest or ambition could fill them; but it was every inch of it let out in lodgings for his friends.

The Life of Alexander Pope, London, 1769, pp. 475-6, 479, 485.

SAMUEL JOHNSON (1709-1784)

It does not appear that he lost a single friend by coldness or by injury; those who loved him once, continued their kindness. . . .

By perpetual practice, language had in his mind a systematical arrangement; having always the same use for words, he had words so selected and combined as to be ready at his call. . . .

He consulted his friends and listened with great willingness to criticism; and, what was of more importance, he consulted himself and let nothing pass against his own judgment. . . .

Praises have been accumulated on *The Rape of the Lock* by readers of every class, from the critic to the chambermaid. . . . New things are made familiar and familiar things are made new. . . .

He cultivated our language with so much diligence and art that he has left in his *Homer* a treasure of poetical elegances to posterity. His version may be said to have tuned the English tongue. . . .

New sentiments and new images others may produce; but to attempt any further improvement of versification will be dangerous. Art and diligence have now done their best and what shall be added will be the effort of tedious toil and needless curiosity. . . . If Pope be not a poet, where is poetry to be found?

The Lives of the English Poets, 1779 and 1781, World's Classics ed., London, 1906, repr. 1942, pp. 317, 321, 331–2, 335, 344.

WILLIAM LISLE BOWLES (1762-1850)

No-one can stand pre-eminent as a great Poet, unless he has not only a heart susceptible of the most pathetic or most exalted feelings of Nature, but an eye *attentive to* and *familiar with* every external appearance that she may exhibit, in every change of season, every variation of light and shade, every rock, every tree, every leaf, in her solitary places . . . Here Pope, from infirmities, and from physical causes, was particularly deficient. . . . With weak eyes and tottering strength, it is physically impossible he could be a *descriptive* Bard . . . But how different, how minute his descriptions when he describes what he is master of: for instance, the game of Ombre in the *Rape of the Lock*. This is from artificial life; and with artificial life, from his infirmities, he must have been chiefly conversant. But if he had been gifted with the same powers of observing outward Nature, I have no doubt he would have evinced as much accuracy in describing the appropriate and peculiar beauties such as Nature exhibits in the Forest where he lived, as he was able to describe, in a manner so novel, and with colours so vivid, a Game of Cards.

'Concluding Observations on the Poetic Character of Pope', in *The Works of Alexander Pope*, ed. W. L. Bowles, London, 1806, vol. X, pp. 370–2.

I will briefly state the course of my argument. . . . 1st. *Works of Nature* . . . are *more* sublime and beautiful than works of art; therefore more poetical. 2nd. The passions of the human heart . . . are more *poetical* than *artificial manners*. 3rd. The great poet of human passions is the most consummate master of his art. . . . 4th. If these premises are true, the descriptive poet, who paints external nature, is more poetical . . . than the painter of external circumstances in *artificial life*, as . . . Pope [paints] a game of cards!

The Invariable Principles of Poetry, London, 1819, p. 22.

PERCIVAL STOCKDALE (1736-1811)

The Elysian Fields of Pope on which we are now going to enter, where we shall meet with every object that can soothe, and charm the mind; with every object that can excite its finest emotions, its noblest agitations. Here the judgment, the taste, the spirit of a great master speaks, with united force to your reason, to your sentiments, to your best affections, to your sublimest passions. Here is plan and system, directing boldness and fire with an easy, happy, and imperceptible control. Here you enjoy an exuberant variety; where all the objects give expression to one another; you powerfully feel the effect, but the design is not obtruded on you. . . .

We are told by that gentleman Warton that 'Pope's close and constant reasoning had imparted and crushed the faculty of imagination.' Good God! What a preposterous assertion is this! . . . No, Dr Warton; the reasoning faculty is the essence the vigorous and exalting stem, of the immaterial and immortal man. Reason supplies the ambrosial nutrition and the force which produce the ramifications and the blossoms of imagination.

Lectures on the Truly Eminent English Poets, 2 vols., London, 1807, vol. I, pp. 406, 437, 440.

WILLIAM WORDSWORTH (1770-1850)

Pope bewitched the nation by his melody and dazzled it by his polished style, and was himself blinded by his own success. Having wandered from humanity in his Eclogues, with boyish inexperience, the praise which the compositions obtained, tempted him into a belief that nature was not to be trusted, at least in pastoral poetry.

'Essay Supplementary to the Preface' [to the *Lyrical Ballads*], in *Poems*, London 1815, 2 vols., vol. I, p. 356.

SAMUEL TAYLOR COLERIDGE (1772-1834)

Among those with whom I conversed, there were, of course, very many who had formed their taste and their notions of poetry from the writings of Mr Pope and his followers. . . . I was not blind to the merits of this school, yet as . . . they gave me little pleasure, I doubtless undervalued the *kind*, and, with the presumption of youth, witheld from its masters the legitimate name of poets. . . . I saw that the excellence of this kind consisted in just and acute observations on men and manners in an artificial state of society as its matter and substance— and in the logic of wit conveyed in smooth and strong epigrammatic

couplets as its form.... The matter and diction seemed to me
characterized not so much by poetic thoughts as by thoughts *translated*
into the language of poetry.

Biographia Literaria, 1817, Everyman Revised ed., London, 1960,
p. 9.

WILLIAM HAZLITT (1778-1830)

He was not ... distinguished as a poet of lofty enthusiasm, of strong
imagination, with a passionate sense of the beauties of nature, or a
deep insight into the workings of the heart; but he was a wit, and a
critic, a man of sense, of observation, and the world, with a keen relish
for the elegances of art, or of nature when embellished by art, a quick
tact for propriety of thought and manners as established by the forms
and customs of society, a refined sympathy with the sentiments and
habitudes of human life, as he felt them within the little circle of his
family and friends. He was in a word, the poet not of nature but of
art.... He was the poet of personality and of polished life.... The
fashion of the day bore sway in his mind over the immutable law of
nature. He preferred the artificial to the natural in external objects...
[and] in passion....
His mind was the antithesis of strength and grandeur; its power
was the power of indifference. He had none of the enthusiasm of
poetry; he was in poetry what the sceptic is in religion.

Lectures on the English Poets, 1818, New Universal Library ed.,
London, 1908, pp. 109, 111.

THOMAS CAMPBELL (1777-1844)

Pope was neither so insensible to the beauties of nature, nor so in-
distinct in describing them as to forfeit the character of a genuine
poet.... I would beg leave to observe ... that the faculty by which a
poet luminously describes objects of art is essentially the same faculty
which enables him to be a faithful describer of simple nature....
Why, then, try Pope or any other poet, exclusively by his powers of
describing inanimate phenomena? Nature, in the wide and proper
sense of the word, means life in all its circumstances—nature moral as
well as external.... Pope's discrimination lay in the lights and shades
of human manners, which are at least as interesting as those of rocks
and leaves.

Essay on the English Poets, 1819, 3rd ed. London, 1848, pp. 110,
111, 116.

B

GEORGE GORDON BYRON (1788-1824)

It is this very harmony . . . in Pope, which has raised the vulgar and atrocious cant against him—because his versification is perfect, it is assumed that it is his only perfection; because his truths are so clear, it is asserted that he has no invention; and because he is always intelligible it is taken for granted that he has no genius. We are sneeringly told that he is the Poet of Reason as if this was a reason for his being no poet. Taking passage for passage, I will undertake to cite more lines teeming with *imagination* from Pope than from any *two* living poets, be they who they may.

'Some Observations upon an Article in Blackwood's Magazine,' 1820, *Letters and Journals*, ed. R. E. Prothero, London, 1900, vol. IV, App. IX, p. 489.

Art is *not* inferior to nature for poetical purposes. What makes a regiment of soldiers a more noble object of view than the same mass of mob? Their arms, their dresses, their banners, and the *art* and artificial symmetry of their position and movements. A Highlander's plaid, a Mussulman's turban, and a Roman toga, are more poetical than the tattooed or untattooed buttocks of a New Sandwich savage, although they were described by William Wordsworth himself like the 'idiot in his glory'. . . .

Mr Bowles makes the chief part of a ship's poesy depend upon the 'wind': then why is a ship under sail more poetical than a hog in a high wind? The hog is all nature, the ship is all art. . . .

Pope is the moral poet of all civilization; and as such, let us hope that he will one day be the national poet of mankind. He is the only poet who never shocks; the only poet whose faultlessness has been made his reproach. Cast your eye over his productions; consider their extent and contemplate their variety;—pastoral, passion, mock-heroic, translation, satire, ethics,—all excellent and often perfect.

Letter to [John Murray] on the Rev W. L. Bowles' Strictures on the Life and Writings of Pope, 1821, 3rd ed. London, 1821, pp. 34–5, 54–5.

ROBERT SOUTHEY (1774-1843)

The age of Pope was the golden age of poets—but it was the pinchbeck age of poetry. They flourished in the sunshine of private and public patronage. The art meantime was debased, and it continued to be so as long as Pope continued Lord of the ascendant. . . .

The mischief was effected not by his satirical and moral pieces, ...
it was by his *Homer*. There have been other versions as unfaithful;
but none were ever so well executed in as bad a style; and no other
work in the language so greatly vitiated the diction of English poetry.
Common readers ... will always be taken by glittering faults, as larks
are caught by bits of looking glass: and in this meretricious translation, the passages that were most unlike the original, which were most
untrue to nature, and therefore most false in taste, were precisely those
which were most applauded and on which critic after critic dwelt
with one cuckoo note of admiration. ... The art of poetry, or rather the
art of versification, which was now the same thing, was 'made easy to
the meanest capacity'.

The Life and Works of William Cowper, London, 1836, vol. II,
pp. 141-2.

THOMAS DE QUINCEY (1785-1859)

The Satires [and Moral Epistles] ... were of false origin. They
arose in a sense of talent for caustic effects, unsupported by any satiric
heart. Pope had neither the malice ... nor the deep moral indignation. ... He was contented enough with society as he found it:
bad it might be, but it was good enough for *him*. ... It provokes fits
of laughter, in a man who knows Pope's real nature, to watch him in the
process of brewing the storm that spontaneously will not come;
whistling, like a mariner, for a wind to fill his satiric sails; and pumping
up into his face hideous grimaces in order to appear convulsed with
histrionic rage. Pope should have been counselled never to write satire,
except on those evenings when he was suffering horribly from indi-
gestion. By this means indignation would have been ready made. The
rancour against all mankind would have been sincere; and there would
have needed to be no extra expense in getting up the steam. As it is,
the short puffs of anger, the uneasy snorts of fury in Pope's satire,
give one painfully the feeling of a locomotive-engine with unsound
lungs.

Essay in *North British Review*, August, 1848. Reprinted in
Collected Writings, ed. David Masson, Edinburgh, 1890, vol. XI,
pp. 68-9.

We ... believe that in Pope lay a disposition radically noble and
generous, clouded and overshadowed by superficial foibles. ... He was
not mean, little minded, indirect, splenetic, vindictive and morose.

Article in the 7th ed. of the *Encyclopoedia Britannica,* 1842. Reprinted in *Collected Writings,* ed. David Masson, Edinburgh, 1890,
vol. IV, p. 276.

JOHN RUSKIN (1819-1900)

I have brought my little volume of Pope's poems with me, which
I shall read carefully. I hardly know which is most remarkable—the
magnificent power and precision of mind—or the miserable corruption
of the entire element in which it is educated—and the flatterings—
falsenesses—affectations—and indecencies, which divert the purpose
and waste the strength of the writer, while his natural perception of
truth and his carefully acquired knowledge of humanity still render
his works of inestimable value—I see he was first educated by a
Roman Catholic—and then in *Twickenham* classicism—I am glad to
find my term is exactly what I wanted it to be—Pope is the purest
example, as well as the highest, of the Cockney classic.

Letter to his father, 1851, in *Letters from Venice,* ed. J. L. Bradley,
New Haven, 1955, p. 12.

MATTHEW ARNOLD (1822-1888)

We are to regard Dryden as the puissant and glorious founder, Pope
as the splendid high priest, of our age of prose and reason, of our excellent and indispensable eighteenth century.... Do you ask me
whether Dryden's verse, take it almost where you will, is not good?

> A milk-white Hind, immortal and unchanged,
> Fed on the lawns and in the forest ranged.

I answer: Admirable for the purposes of the inaugurator of an age of
prose and reason. Do you ask me whether Pope's verse, take it almost
where you will, is not good?

> To Hounslow Heath I point, and Banstead Down;
> Thence comes your mutton, and these
>   chicks my own.

I answer: Admirable for the purposes of the high priest of an age of
prose and reason. But do you ask me whether such verse proceeds from
men with an adequate poetic criticism of life, from men whose criticism
of life has a high seriousness, or even, without that high seriousness,
has poetic largeness, freedom, insight, benignity? Do you ask me
whether the application of ideas to life in the verse of these men, often
a powerful application, no doubt, is a powerful *poetic* application?

Do you ask me whether the poetry of these men has either the matter or the inseparable manner of such an adequate poetic criticism; whether it has the accent of

>   Absent thee from felicity awhile . . .

or of

>   And what is else not to be overcome . . .

or of

>   O martyr sounded in virginitee!

I answer: It has not and cannot have them; it is the poetry of the builders of an age of prose and reason. Though they may write in verse, though they may in a certain sense be masters of the art of versification, Dryden and Pope are not classics of our poetry, they are classics of our prose.

'The Study of Poetry', 1880, in *Essays in Criticism*, 1st and 2nd series, Everyman, revised ed., London, 1964, pp. 252-3.

LESLIE STEPHEN (1832-1904)

Pope was governed by the instantaneous feeling. His emotion came in sudden jets and gushes, instead of a continuous stream. The same peculiarity deprives his poetry of continuous harmony or profound unity of conception. . . . But on the other hand he can perceive admirably all that can be seen at a glance from a single point of view. Though he could not be continuous, he could return again and again to the same point; he could polish, correct, eliminate superfluities, and compress his meaning more and more closely, till he has constructed short passages of imperishable excellence. . . . He corrects and prunes too closely. . . . But the injury is compensated by the singular terseness and vivacity of his best style. . . .

Pope's best writing . . . is the essence of conversation. It has the quick movement, the boldness and brilliance which we suppose to be attributes of the best talk. . . .

Pope is undoubtedly monotonous. Except in one or two lyrics . . . he invariably employed the same metre. The discontinuity of his style, and the strict rules which he adopted, tend to distintegrate his poems. They are a series of brilliant passages, often of brilliant couplets, stuck together in a conglomerate; and as the inferior connecting matter decays, the interstices open and allow the whole to fall into ruin. . . . Making full allowance for Pope's monotony and the tiresome prominence of certain mechanical effects, we must, I think, admit that he

has after all succeeded in doing with unsurpassable excellence what
innumerable rivals have failed to do as well. The explanation is ...
that he was a man of genius.

Alexander Pope, London, 1880, pp. 189, 194, 197, 199.

JOHN MIDDLETON MURRY (1889-1957)

... It seems that Collins could have expressed anything, so rich was
his technical endowment; yet that endowment came near preventing
him from having anything to express at all. One perfect poem, and
one only, lifts him out of the ranks of the minor poets; he can only
just support the posthumous renown heaped upon him by a tradition
of criticism which is unduly impatient of Pope and the Augustans.
Collins brings a breath of a diviner fragrance, it has been said over and
over again; but is it—save in the one great poem—really more divine?
To safeguard ourselves against an ecstasy of wonder at this phœnix
in the desert of the eighteenth century, we need to remember—what
is too easily forgotten—what Pope could do and did, to reconsider for
a moment passages such as these two from *The Unfortunate Lady*:—

> Most souls, 'tis true, but peep out once an age,
> Dull sullen prisoners in the body's cage:
> Dim lights of life, that burn a length of years,
> Useless, unseen, as lamps in sepulchres;
> Like Eastern kings a lazy state they keep
> And close confined to their own palace sleep ...

> What tho' no sacred earth allow thee room,
> Nor hallow'd dirge be uttered o'er thy tomb?
> Yet shall thy grave with rising flowers be dressed
> And the green turf lie lightly on thy breast:
> There shall the morn her earliest tears bestow,
> There the first roses of the year shall blow;
> While angels with their silver wings o'ershade
> The ground now sacred by thy reliques made ...

The second of these passages is on a favourite theme of Collins. It
appears in the *Dirge for Cymbeline*, in the *Ode to Thomson,* in the
stanzas to the memory of Colonel Ross, and in *How Sleep the Brave*.
But only in the last does Collins achieve an expression that is equal to
Pope's. In the *Ode to Thomson*, for instance, he writes:—

> The year's best sweets shall duteous rise
> To deck its poet's sylvan grave.

That is really almost as far from Pope's couplet, 'Yet shall thy grave,' as it is from Shakespeare's 'I'll sweeten thy sad grave.' It is on an altogether different plane. In *How Sleep the Brave*, it is true, Collins reaches the level of Pope in his handling of the theme.

> When spring with dewy fingers cold
> Returns to deck their hallowed mould,
> She there shall dress a sweeter sod
> Than fancy's feet have ever trod.

Perhaps the purity of the phrase 'with dewy fingers cold' lifts those lines by an almost imperceptible degree above the lines of Pope; but it is the fraction of a degree, no more. In treating the commonplace of nature Pope and Collins were on a level. But the earlier lines we have quoted from *The Unfortunate Lady*, 'Most souls, 'tis true . . .' are of a kind and excellence beyond Collins's range. They touch the intensity and psychological revelation of Donne, and have a sustained perfection of phrasing that Donne never attained.

We may crudely state the relative position thus: if we take away from Collins the *Ode to Evening*, his remaining excellence would be comfortably contained in a third of Pope's excellence, for besides the commonplace of Nature, Pope was also a master of Wit in the best Metaphysical sense—namely, the striking expression of deep psychological perceptions, the power which could

> the deep knowledge of dark truths so teach
> That sense might judge what fancy could not reach—

and of wit in the Augustan sense, the verbal epigram of an alert mind. . . .

Countries of the Mind, London, 1922, pp. 86-8.

LYTTON STRACHEY (1880-1932)

. . . If we are to understand . . . that, in Matthew Arnold's opinion, no poetic criticism of life can be adequate unless it possesses largeness, freedom, and benignity, we must certainly agree that Pope's poetic criticism of life was far from adequate; for his way of writing was neither large nor free, and there was nothing benignant about him. . . .

Perhaps the most characteristic of all the elements in the couplet is antithesis. Ordinary regularity demands that the sense should end with every line—that was a prime necessity; but a more scrupulous symmetry would require something more—a division of the line itself into two halves, whose meanings should correspond. And yet a further refinement was possible: each half might be again divided, and the

corresponding divisions in the two halves might be so arranged as to
balance each other. The force of neatness could no further go; and
thus the most completely evolved type of the heroic line is one composed of four main words arranged in pairs, so as to form a double
antithesis.

'Willing to wound and yet afraid to strike' is an example of such a
line. . . . With astonishing ingenuity he builds up these exquisite structures, in which the parts are so cunningly placed that they seem to
interlock spontaneously, and, while they are all formed on a similar
model, are yet so subtly adjusted that they produce a fresh pleasure
as each one appears. But that is not all. Pope was pre-eminently a
satirist. . . . Civilization illuminated by animosity—such was his theme;
such was the passionate and complicated material from which he wove
his patterns of balanced precision and polished clarity. Antithesis
penetrates below the structure; it permeates the whole conception of
his work. Fundamental opposites clash, and are reconciled. The pro-
fundities of persons, the futilities of existences, the rage and spite of
genius—these things are mixed together, and presented to our eyes in
the shape of a Chinese box. . . . His poetic criticism of life was, simply
and solely, the heroic couplet. . . .

Pope, The Leslie Stephen Lecture for 1925, Cambridge, 1925,
pp. 13–14, 23–6.

EDITH SITWELL (1887-1964)

. . . Before we examine the life history of the small, unhappy, tortured
creature, who is one of the greatest of our poets, and who is, in his two
finest poems, perhaps the most flawless artist our race has produced,
it will be better to examine the prevailing attitude towards his
poetry. . . .

The reputation of Pope is safe among the poets of this time; but it
is a fact, also, that a large section of the public has not yet recovered
from the cold, damp mossiness that has blighted the public taste for the
last fifty or even sixty years; and to these people, Pope is not one of the
greatest of our poets, one of the most lovable of men, but a man who
was deformed in spirit as in body. . . . This general blighting and
withering of the poetic taste is the result of the public mind having
been overshadowed by such Aberdeen-granite tombs and monuments
as Matthew Arnold—is the result, also, of the substitution of scholar
for poet, of school inspector for artist. . . .

Never was a man worthier of love than this most misunderstood man,
this great and—at his best—flawless poet. . . . He had, perhaps, the
most subtle and sensitive feeling for beauty of form possessed by any

artist that our race has produced; yet he realized ... that his own outward form raised feelings of mocking amusement or coarse pity in the
beholders. ...

Alexander Pope, London, 1930, pp. 1–2, 7, 8.

WILLIAM EMPSON (1906–   )

... There is also the ambiguity which talks about one thing and implies several ways of judging or feeling about it. ... Pope continually
makes use of it; partly because, though himself a furious partisan
(or rather because of it, so as to pretend he is being fair), he externa-
lizes his remarks very completely into statements of fact such as must
always admit of two judgments; partly because his statements are so
compact, and his rhythmic unit so brief, that he has not always room
for an unequivocal expression of feeling. The word 'equivocal' is a good
one here; much of the force of his satire comes from its pretence of
equity. He stimulates the reader's judgment by leaving an apparently
unresolved duality in his own—'this is the truth about my poor friend,
and you may laugh if you will.' The now fashionable attitude to the
eighteenth century rather tends to obscure this point; it is true the
humour of the period is often savage, but that does not show that the
judgments with which it is concerned are crude.

Is Pope sneering or justifying, for instance, in one of the best known
of these spare but widely buttressed constructions?—

> who, high in Drury Lane,
> Lulled by soft zephyrs through the broken pane,
> Rhymes e'er he wakes, and prints before term ends,
> Obliged by hunger, and request of friends.
> (*Epistle to Arbuthnot.*)

No one can deny that these words ridicule, but: *obliged by hunger*:
I am not sure that they titter; it is only after you have been faced with
the dignity of human need that you are moved on to see the grandeur
of human vanity. Much recent apologetic for Pope has contented itself with saying how clever it was of the little fellow to be so rude; but
to suppose this line means merely 'the man must have been a fool as
well as a bore, since he was hungry,' is not merely an injustice
to Pope's humanity, it is a failure to understand the tone he adopts
towards his readers.

> Soft were my numbers, who could take offence
> When pure description held the place of sense? ...
> Yet then did Gildon draw his venal quill.
> I wished the man a dinner, and sat still.
> (*Epistle to Arbuthnot.*)

Good, sympathetic Mr Pope, one is to think; he has a profound knowledge of human nature. The situation in these two examples is the same; the first stresses his contempt, the second his magnanimity; but in neither can one be sure what proportions are intended. . . .

There may be an interest due to the contrast between the stock response and the response demanded by the author. I think myself, in the following border-line case, that I am describing the attitude of Pope, but such an analysis would have achieved its object if it described the attitude only of the majority of his readers. It is that description of a great eighteenth-century mansion in which Pope is apparently concerned only to make its grandeur seem vulgar and stupid.

>   his building is a town,
> His pond an ocean, his parterre a down.
> Who but must laugh, the master when he sees,
> A puny insect, shuddering at a breeze. . . .
>
> My lord advances, with majestic mien,
> Smit with the mighty pleasure to be seen. . . .
>
> But hark, the chiming clocks to dinner call;
> A hundred footsteps scrape the marble hall: . . .
>
> Is this a dinner? this a genial room?
> No, 'tis a temple, and a hecatomb.
>   (*Moral Essays,* iv.)

All this is great fun; but before concluding that Pope's better judgment really disapproved of the splendour that he evidently envied, one must remember the saying that as Augustus found Rome, so Dryden found English 'brick, and left it marble'; that the Augustans minded about architecture and what Augustus did; that a great part of the assurance and solidity of their attitude to life depended on solid contemporary evidence of national glory. When Pope prophesies the destruction of the building his language takes on a grandeur which reflects back and transfigures it:

> Another age shall see the golden ear
> Embrown the slope, and nod on the parterre,
> Deep harvest bury all his pride has planned,
> And laughing Ceres reassume the land.

These lines seem to me to convey what is called an intuitive intimacy with nature; one is made to see a cornfield as something superb and as old as humanity, and breaking down dykes irresistibly, like the sea. But, of course, it *embrowns* as with further more universal, *gilding,* and *nods on the parterre* like a duchess; common things are made dignified by a mutual comparison which entirely depends on the dignity of Canons. The glory is a national rather than a personal one; democracy will *bury* the oligarch; but the national glory is now centred in the oligarch; and if the whole people has been made great, it is through the greatness of the Duke of Chandos.

This seems to me rather a curious example of the mutual comparison which elevates both parties; in this case, it is the admiration latent in a sneer which becomes available as a source of energy for these subsidiary uses: and also an example of how the Wordsworthian feeling for nature can be called forth not by an isolated and moping interest in nature on her own account, but by a conception of nature in terms of human politics. I hope, at any rate, you agree with me that the lines convey this sort of sympathy intensely; that there is some sense of the immensity of harvest through a whole country; that the relief with which the cripple for a moment identifies himself with something so strong and generous gives these two couplets an extraordinary scale. ...

Seven Types of Ambiguity, London, 1930, 2nd ed. (rev.) 1947, pp. 125-8.

GEOFFREY TILLOTSON (1905-   )

... The value of correctness in or out of the heroic couplet lies first of all in the effect it has on the reader's attitude. When a reader finds that his poet considers himself responsible for every syllable not simply in this or that poem but in every poem of his entire works, then his alertness is intensified, his curiosity aroused, his trust increased. Here, he sees, is a poet who will set him in a motion which will only change as a dance changes, not as a walk on ice changes. Correctness elicits and does not abuse the reader's confidence. The reader will, however, soon tire if nothing happens to show how strong his confidence is. Once he can trust his poet, he looks to have the steadfastness of his trust proved and deepened by variety of experience. Pope satisfies this expectation in a thousand ways. Pope's practice is to provide expectation rather than surprise. But the expectation is expectation *of* surprise. The reader of Pope anticipates perfect responsibility syllable by syllable, and awaits the changes which will show that the responsibility is being put to advantage. The thousand surprises come and they enchant all the more because, as certainly as rime in a known stanza, they have been subconsciously anticipated. ...

The problem for the critic of Pope's poetry is that of relating the mechanics of the verse to its quality for the emotions. This emotional quality is felt by many readers, though not by all. Often the failure to experience it is due to unfamiliarity with Pope's poetry, persistence in thinking of him as a poet of *sententiae*. Pope's fame as a gnomic writer has often proved a barrier to his fame as a poetical poet. It has attracted the wrong readers and kept away the right ones. Pope did not proclaim as his favourite line:

> A *little learning* is a dang'rous thing.

The couplet he did single out was one which most pleased his ear, the one indeed which Keats might have chosen for him

> Lo! where Mæotis sleeps, and hardly flows
> The freezing Tanais thro' a waste of snows.

Pope states that he chose verse as the medium for the *Essay on Man* for reasons which he enumerates, but he knew that the material was, apart from those reasons, mainly material for prose. He should not be judged by his *Essay on Man* or the *Essay on Criticism*, though even in these works the poetry has been underrated. Nor must he be judged by his *Pastorals and Windsor Forest*, unless the judge will qualify his sentence by understanding into what context of historical principles these poems fall. Nor must he be judged on the *Rape of the Lock* unless the judge, before he begins to judge, will understand that because a poem is about the work of a pair of scissors on a lock of hair it is not therefore necessarily a trivial poem. (We have heard too much about the 'delicate filigree' of that poem.) Nor must Pope be judged by his 'pathetic' pieces—that is, the pieces more directly addressed to the emotions—unless the judge understands that his method of writing in these poems is often one of hiding emotion away, of saying indirectly what he felt. Pope set himself against the Elizabethan methods of writing passionate poetry, which in turn became those of the nineteenth century. He did not go directly to work crying out with Shakespeare (in the sonnets) or Donne that his heart was feeling this and that grief or rapture. When, at the close of *Eloisa to Abelard,* Pope tells a woman—it is probably Lady Mary Wortley Montagu—that he loves her, he says it by means of a picture of other lovers; and, moreover, by means of other lovers whom Eloisa imagines as hoping that they will never love as she and Abelard loved—the twofold indirection of Eloisa's vision of two other lovers made threefold by a negative. His profoundest love-poem is given the form of an imitation of one of Horace's odes. He may speak his less passionate emotion directly, but it is controlled before he begins. We know from a hundred independent sources that Pope had the true fire in him, but he did not set it before the reader's eyes as a bare flame. He set it instead to turn

> ... ev'ry wheel of that unweary'd Mill
> That turn'd ten thousand verses ...

... Pope's methods of touching the reader's passions, of arousing his emotional response, were mainly those of clear statement,

Something in Verse as true as Prose,

poetry, as Crabbe put it, without an atmosphere. He had no use for
poetry or prose which aroused the emotions only at the expense of
divorcing them from intelligence, reason and Nature, and leading them
off in a round of bedazzlement and inebriety. And he disliked equally
the poetry of some of Donne's followers in which the intelligence is so
much teased that the emotions are left unaffected. Yet he partly re-
sembled the metaphysicals, since he was out to offer something of
value to the understanding. To make his kind of poetry he relied partly
on the intellectual quality of what he was saying. And his poetry serves
to demonstrate the proximity, the interpenetrableness, of the intellect
and the emotions. . . .

From *On The Poetry of Pope*, Oxford, 1938, rev. ed. 1950, pp. 115–
16, 160–4. Footnotes have been omitted.

G. WILSON KNIGHT (1897-   )

[In *Windsor Forest*] the descriptions, being inward, penetrate to
the dynamic centres of life, and give, without effort, pictorial quality
and action, as in the well-known

> See! from the brake the whirring pheasant springs,
> And mounts exulting on triumphant wings:
> Short is his joy; he feels the fiery wound,
> Flutters in blood, and panting beats the ground.
> Ah! what avail his glossy, varying dyes,
> His purple crest, and scarlet-circled eyes,
> The vivid green his shining plumes unfold,
> His painted wings, and breast that flames with gold? (111)

Rich as is the description, the phrases work in obedience to a whole
drawn directly from the energies of nature. Each image is apt, but none
superlative. There is a reserve of power and a poetic humility; that is,
power is felt in the conception, not just the expression. The regularity
of couplet-rhyme helps in checking all separate excellences, levelling
and subduing them, with a corresponding release to the central experience, while poignant action informs a poetic tranquillity; as in
[the earlier] phrase 'waving prospect', where the still and vast abstract
conception checks the more lively movement which is somehow then
enclosed in stillness. . . .
    Pope's animal apprehension is one with animal sympathy. The de-
struction of bird-life is again vigorously imagined when a fowler is
described roving with 'slaughterous gun' in winter:

He lifts the tube, and levels with his eye:
Straight a short thunder breaks the frozen sky:
Oft, as in airy rings they skim the heath,
The clam'rous lapwings feel the leaden death:
Oft, as the mounting larks their notes prepare,
They fall, and leave their little lives in air. (129) . . .

A whole experience is given, an authentic instant of actual existence,
a piece of a living universe. The realization is stark, sudden, and unerring; as, too, in the phrase 'leaden death'. 'Clamorous' and
'mounting' are careful epithets, and 'little' denotes the sympathy implicit throughout; with a clever silhouetting of life's mystery in the
thought of its loss, the birds as tiny flamelets puffed out in song.
Animals are inwardly felt, as in the 'ready spaniel' shown 'panting
with hope' (99–100) or the 'impatient courser' ('courser' because he is
felt as dynamic) seen as excited in 'every vein', pawing the ground
and tingling for 'the distant plain' (151). The animal's power and swiftness is admirably caught in 'earth rolls back beneath the flying steed'
(158), the phrase aiming to net the paradoxical quality of speed.
Animals are usually created in their vital and peculiar movement from
an inward sympathy comparable with Shakespeare's, and continuous
with the apprehension of dynamic quality, as well as shape and colour,
in nature generally. . . .

The poem expands further, Windsor Forest becoming a national
symbol, one with 'Britannia's goddess', Liberty (91–2). Oaks are
'future navies' (222), with no straining of association. An Elizabethan
royalism is recaptured, Windsor boasting in Queen Anne 'as bright a
goddess and as chaste a queen' as Diana in 'old Arcadia'; at once pro-
tectress of the 'sylvan scene', 'earth's fair light', and 'empress of the
main' (159–64). So the courtier ranks above the poet, whose 'chymic
art' reading magic lore from nature and history is a brilliantly
characterized second (235–56). The Thames recalls past nobilities,
river-feelings forming organically among the paradisal, yet contemporary, impressions. Again, as in the days of Elizabeth, 'discord' has
been quelled, only this time by 'great Anna'; while the 'sacred' blessings
of a peaceful reign are expected, with the building of 'temples' re-
placing civil war and bloodshed (321–78). England is finally seen as
supreme arbiter and 'great oracle' of the world (382). All evils are to be
stilled on that day when

Unbounded Thames shall flow for all mankind. (398) . . .

Pope expects his country to oppose 'slavery' (408). He proclaims the
end of conquest (408) and ambition (416) with the advent of universal peace.

This felt organic continuity of nature, animal-life, and human civilization is most important. It is not a logical sequence; my quotations are drawn from various parts of what may well seem an untidy poem. The form is inherently, not studiously, organic. The generalizing tendency never loses contact with perceptual impressions. . . . *Windsor Forest* is felt as a teeming world: there are no limits to its boundaries. We are pointed on, through thoughts of imperial expansion as creatively interlocking one's own country with a great human whole, to the 'naked youths' (405) of America. . . . Evils are keenly remembered: the forest's past as a setting for savagery and oppression (43–92) is set beside its present placidity and expected future. Such Shakespearian inclusiveness, covering a number of geographical references, points towards the *Essay on Man*. Pope's life-work is rooted in *Windsor Forest* it holds the germ of all the rest, the satires too. . . . Nature and man are again in partnership: which recaptured sense of harmony is reflected into an assured poetic ease, the rose-chain and bowery prison of the couplet. . . .

'The Vital Flame: An Essay on Pope' in *The Burning Oracle*, London, 1939, pp. 132–6.

CRITICS ON POPE SINCE 1940

JOHN BUTT

The Man and the Poet

... In so far as anyone can resolve what character he will choose to exhibit to the world, Pope had resolved upon the character of the Good Man. . . . There can be little doubt that Pope designed the publication of his letters to exhibit this view of the dutiful son, the kind-thoughted friend, the well-bred host, the disinterested critic of society, yet warm in wishes for his country's good and patient under attack: in short, the man of plain living, high thinking and unimpeachable integrity. This is the view of himself that he discovered in his letters as he reread them, rather than the view that he designedly wrote into them. Not every critic of Pope in his own day or since has been able to see him in this light; and when allowance has been made for contemporary malice and subsequent prejudice, it must be admitted that his moral character was not perfect. He can be convicted of equivocation and of devious dealing; and though he was slow in replying to attacks, and not infrequently forgave the injuries done him, he hit harder than perhaps his profession as a Christian permitted; he hit hard, but deftly, in an age of hard hitting.

But though I think that his moral character has been unduly impugned, it is not my present purpose to defend it. Of greater interest is his employment of the character he had chosen. He had decided that goodness should be the profession of his mature years just as he had decided that wit was to be the profession of his youth. Doubtless he was aware from time to time that he did not always succeed in living up to his profession, just as a Christian is aware of committing sin; but either he had lived so long with his *persona* that he failed to recognize the mask he carried, or he was unable to abandon what had become the inspiration of his poetry.

c

He was as much accustomed as his friend Swift to the use of a *persona* in his writings. He had taught himself to write by imitating the styles of different masters, and most of his earliest surviving verses bear witness to his habit: 'Of a Lady singing to her lute; in imitation of Waller', for example, or 'To the author of a Poem entitled Successio, in imitation of the Earl of Dorset'; and though the famous 'Ode on Solitude' bears no similar subtitle, it is clearly intended as an exercise in the manner of Cowley on the popular theme of 'The Happy Man'. No one is misled by these straightforward adoptions of a poetic *persona*, and of others equally straightforward in such poems as 'Eloisa to Abelard' and 'The Dying Christian to his Soul'. But beginning with the 'Epistle to Miss Blount with the Works of Voiture', which probably belongs to the year 1710, and continuing in some later verse epistles, that 'to Miss Blount, on her leaving the Town, after the Coronation' (1714), 'to Mr Jervas, with Drydens Translations of Fresnoy's Art of Painting' (1715), 'to Mr Gay' (1720), the noble epistle to the Earl of Oxford, with the poems of Parnell (1722) and the affectionate verses 'To Mrs M. B. on her Birthday' (1723)—in all these poems there is evident a *persona* that is clearly intended to resemble the features of the historical Alexander Pope. Accustomed as he was to model himself upon verse precedent, it is not unlikely that Pope had his models here, too; and they are not far to seek. There were the urbane verse epistles of Dryden to Sir Godfrey Kneller and to his 'dear friend Mr Congreve'; and behind Dryden was the urbanity of Horace. In learning to adjust his features to the mask of Horace, Pope discovered a set of countenance and a manner of behaviour that he felt suited him best of all; the April weather of his mind was allowed to settle at last into an Horatian midsummer. Early eighteenth-century society dictated its own modifications of the Horatian pattern. The predominant masculinity of Dryden's and Horace's epistles were not altogether suited to a society where women had begun to take a more prominent place. . . .

We may watch the features settling both in Pope's letters and in his poems. The reason why the process can be watched in his poetry is that as the time went on he conducted an ever-deepening exploration of his personality. His first massively personal intrusion into his own poetry is in 'The Farewell to London' (1715), where 'the gayest valetudinaire, most thinking rake alive' sees himself against the background of a gay society frequenting theatres and coffee-houses; and from 1730 onwards there are few of his poems in which the poet himself does not take up a prominent position. The *Moral Essays* are one and all conceived as verse epistles, and the same is true of the *Imitations of Horace*, while the presence of an interlocutor in the epistles to Bathurst and Arbuthnot and in the *Epilogue to the Satires*, with their snatches of dialogue, emphasize even more strongly the poet's presence.

The *Essay on Man*, too, is framed within the addresses to Bolingbroke
that open and close the poem. These addresses pay Bolingbroke the
highest of compliments, but they are so arranged that we should see his
associate also. That attractive picture of the two friends setting out on
their shooting expedition:

> Together let us beat this ample field,
> Try what the open, what the covert yield!
> The latent tracts, the giddy heights explore
> Of all who blindly creep, or sightless soar;
> Eye Nature's walks, shoot Folly as it flies,
> And catch the Manners living as they rise:
> Laugh where we must, be candid where we can;
> But vindicate the ways of God to Man—

What purpose does the picture serve but to define the elegant yet
easy spirit of debate in which the discussion will be conducted? It will
be found on examination that every other personal intrusion of the poet
into these later poems, whether he be conversing with friends in his
grotto in the first *Imitation of Horace* or offering them hospitality
at Twickenham in the second, or the scene of domestic irritation with
which the *Epistle of Arbuthnot* opens or the deliberately contrasting
scene of domestic calm at his mother's death-bed with which it closes
—each is designed to control the mood of the poem, and to win the
reader to the poet's point of view.

A wide assortment of factors have combined to produce this very
personal poetry of Pope's maturity. Since 1711 he had been the victim
of unremitting attacks that libelled both his moral character and his
personal appearance. 'If I am not like that,' he seems to have asked
himself, 'what am I like?' And he set himself to correct the libels, encouraged by that sense of self-esteem which fed upon his early success
and helped to determine what character he would choose to exhibit to
the world, not only in verse, but on the canvasses of numerous portrait-
painters and in the busts of Roubiliac and other sculptors, whose work
he seems to have directed with attentive care. Then, too, he had the
example of Horace before him, and a lifetime's practice in poetical
imitation which makes it second nature to adopt a *persona*, as well as
the inheritance of a hundred years of experiment in the Theophrastan
character sketch; and finally, perhaps, at some level of consciousness
there was the recognition that the personality that charmed such a
wide circle of friends could be harnessed to his verse to charm an even
wider circle of readers.

And where in all this is the real man? Professor Maynard Mack, in
an essay called 'The Muse of Satire',[1] has shown how closely modelled

[1] *The Yale Review*, XLI (1951), 80–92. See p. 84 of the present volume.

the poet's *persona* is upon the traditional figure of the satirist. Yet at the same time it is possible to annotate each incident from the satires and show its derivation from the poet's own biography. We are presented with a peculiar blending of the artifact and the real, one of the strangest confusions of life and letters. So accustomed had he become to this blend that Pope himself may not have known how precisely to distinguish the historical portrait from the literary one. That is the enigma that a study of his life and writings offers.

From 'Pope: The Man and the Poet', in *Of Books and Human Kind*, Essays and Poems presented to Bonamy Dobrée, ed. John Butt, London, 1964, pp. 69–79. [The page numbers in this and subsequent footnotes at the end of each essay refer to the *whole* essay, article or chapter.]

S. L. GOLDBERG

Alexander Pope:
The Creative Poet

THE old myth of Pope the personal satirist, the little crooked poet
who reached a kind of greatness by expressing his spite with such
clever 'techniques', is happily dead enough by now. The alternative
myth, of Pope the conscious Augustan prophet, whose greatness is to
voice the ideas and ideals of his age, still survives—partly, no doubt,
because Pope liked to believe in himself. What both miss in him,
of course, or over-simplify, is the creative poet. Neither, for example,
accounts for the combination Leavis has pointed to, of responsiveness
and detachment, hostility and fascination, that quickens his satire
into living poetry. Neither, again, explains why (as various critics have
noted) Pope so frequently dramatizes his own moral position in his
works, or seems ambivalent about the Augustan values he wants to
celebrate. Both myths, in fact, blur important differences of quality
in his work, his difficulties in coming to terms with his material and
the subtle development of his art, for both falsify the relationship
between his consciousness of the world and his consciousness of himself as part of it. The poetic activity in which he discovered the actual
shape of his world and, in that, its ideal possibilities, was the same as
that in which he discovered his own feelings, values, and possible role
as a poet within it. As one matured, so did the other.

A comparatively early poem, the unpretentious little 'Epistle to
Miss Blount... after the Coronation', shows how much he inherited
from the 17th century together with its Metaphysical 'wit'. Its
closest affinities (as so often) are with Marvell: its beautifully light,
sure, teasing intimacy is finer and more moving than Prior, for example; its comparison of urban and country life is more subtly felt,
more exploratory than Cowley. In fact both names only underline the
distinctive self-consciousness it shares with, say, 'The Garden'. Thus
Marvell and Pope both seem fully aware that they stand apart from the
world they live in but must do so in order to seek a balance of its conflicting claims. Moreover, both seem to recognize that the balance they
reach—that delicately embodied in the poem itself—is an ideal that,

for better and worse, ordinary life, always demanding we choose one
way or the other, cannot really support. Each seems aware that his
activity as a poet differs from the activities of other men; but since his
attitude to this is mixed (differing sharply from Romantic glorification),
his poetry seems to gain strength from recognizing just how fragile
and even limited its created order is. . . . One reason why this
'Epistle', with *The Rape of the Lock* perhaps, seems to me the finest
poem Pope wrote before *The Dunciad*, is that here the lively comic
perception, the social gesture and the poetic questioning so meaning-
fully, and with such delightful spontaneity, coincide.

   This is notably *not* the case with other early poems—the 'Elegy
to the Memory of an Unfortunate Lady', for instance, or *Windsor
Forest*, or *Eloisa to Abelard*—where he draws on formal modes from
the 17th century, and naturally sees himself as a Poet in a correspondingly formal way. Nevertheless, I think there are more than
formal reasons why he openly presents himself more or less elaborately in each one of these poems. Under one aspect, we can see them
all as attempting to make conscious to his society the meaning of
Order, Reason, Virtue, Decorum—what it accepted as the various
forms of civilized life. Equally, we can see them as attempting to express the fluid, anarchic energies that both impel and yet threaten
those forms, in the individual and society alike. The two are comple-
mentary sides of all human life of course, just as they are comple-
mentary aspects of poetry as Pope saw it—as in his Prologue to
Addison's *Cato* (1713) or, far more sharply, in the Epistle *To Augustus*
(1737). But clearly, from the very beginning, Pope could hardly avoid
trying to clarify, as central to his whole moral outlook, the relationship
between the chaotic forces of life that he 'feigned' and the conscious
'sense' that he made of it as he did so. The peculiar circumstances of
The Rape of the Lock made the point especially obvious:

>   But since, alas! frail Beauty must decay,
>   Curl'd or uncurl'd, since Locks will turn to grey,
>   Since painted, or not painted, all shall fade,
>   And she who scorns a Man, must die a Maid;
>   What then remains, but well our Pow'r to use,
>   And keep good Humour still whate'er we lose?
>   And trust me, Dear! good Humour can prevail. . . .
>
>   .   .   .   .   .
>
>   When, after Millions slain, your self shall die;
>   When those fair Suns shall sett, as sett they must,
>   And all those Tresses shall be laid in Dust;
>   *This Lock*, the Muse shall consecrate to Fame,
>   And mid'st the Stars inscribe *Belinda's* Name!

Having lightly underscored the universal sexual energies at work in this 'rape', their power over and their final servitude to 'Fate', and the constant human need of viable forms in which to 'use them well', Pope least of all could miss the relevance of all this to his own 'good humoured' activity in the affair. As Reuben Brower in his book on Pope reminds us, within a society that viewed the epic poet—Homer or Virgil—as the great civilizing consciousness of a bygone age, Pope's mock-epic was not entirely mock.

In the 'Elegy', however, he is much more explicit and much less successful. Against the 'glorious' but self-destructive passion of the Lady he tries to place the Poet's more ordered, hence more permanently glorious, 'feigning' of that passion; against the hostile incomprehension of ordinary people, the sympathetic understanding of the Muse; against 'real' life, the Poet's remoteness from it. The trouble is that his imagination slithers about among the possibilities of his material; he relies on a series of merely formal gestures to see him through. What he does seize firmly is the idea of the Lady's burning vitality and the world's coldness towards it: lines 11–46 are the only part of the work that comes to life. The rest of it is hardly more than eloquence in one convention or another. So that when he turns at last from the 'beck'ning ghost' to the Poets who hearken, that is, to placing himself in relation to his material, he achieves only a sad, almost plaintive note—a sense of his own undertaking that chimes perfectly with the 'elegiac' formalities ('hallow'd dirges' and the like), but not with the force with which he had grasped, in rather simple terms but genuinely enough, the Lady's own.

So too with *Eloisa to Abelard*, which is in effect the last and most polished of the 'Ovidian' poems in the late 16th and 17th century. Pope heightens the 'romantic' trappings of the mode to a positively sub-Miltonic degree; on the other hand, he also tries to exploit its Ovidian implications more fully than any Elizabethan (except perhaps for Marlowe and Shakespeare). He uses Eloisa's 'case' as a means of reflecting—often, reflecting upon—the paradoxes and metamorphoses of love; natural desire, with its impulse towards life carrying it into death and its very innocence carrying it into guilt, playing against spiritual desire, which has to take its image and its power from the natural energies it must frustrate. Unlike Milton in *Comus*, Pope does—as Wilson Knight claims—allow the opposing principles full speech. Yet if the actual result can tempt us to define its subject as, so to speak, the Paradox of the Fortunate Disseverance, the reason is that Pope seems to conceive it in these rather theoretical terms himself—as though he could both convey and yet detach himself from the issues only in this way. The poem is repeatedly swamped in waves of rhetorical pathos, deliberate 'tenderness'—in short, by a consciousness once again less able to realize the paradoxical substance

of life than the idea of its paradoxical substance, and which seems
to arise from something that is ominously like *self*-pity and almost
declares itself so in the final lines.

Clearly *Windsor Forest* and *The Rape of the Lock*, with their
more vigorous bite, lie more to the centre of his development, even
though each is limited by a different kind of abstraction. In both
cases, Pope's grasp of his material is less intimate than he supposes.
One sign of this is his tendency to fanciful over-elaboration—with
the sylphs, or the card-game, or some of the mock-heroic machinery
in *The Rape*, for example, or the notorious mythology in *Windsor
Forest*—where his delight in 'treating' these things allows their point
to become diffused. Another is the immaturity of feeling in both
poems. In *Windsor Forest* this appears as a sort of confusion—a confusion that probably has nothing to do with his rewriting of it, though
the last third does little to help. Even within the first eighty lines,
there is an interesting difference between the verse in which he catches
the order of the Eden-like scene before him, as if nature were carefully
composing itself—

> Here waving Groves a checquer'd Scene display . . .
> Thin Trees arise that shun each others Shades . . .
> Ev'n the wild Heath displays her Purple Dies,
> And 'midst the Desart fruitful Fields arise—

and that where he realizes the absence of order:

> . . . O'er Heaps of Ruin stalk'd the stately Hind;
> The Fox obscene to gaping Tombs retires,
> And savage Howlings fill the sacred Quires . . .

Beside the whole of this latter passage, the former seems thin, almost
notional, dependent on deliberately restricted feelings and impressions. The *discordia* seems more convincing than the *concors*. The
strain is even more evident shortly afterwards (ll.93–118), when he
rapidly juxtaposes 'fermenting' youth at the hunt, Albion's eager sons
triumphantly seizing the 'defenceless' town 'with Ease and Plenty
blest', and the pheasant whose exultant power and glory avail him
nothing. We suddenly see hunters and hunted in a vivid but disturbing pattern—disturbing because, despite any *beliefs* about hunting
being a moral substitute for war, it actually puts before our senses
a natural world very different from one where 'tho' all things differ,
all agree' and 'barb'rous Discord' can be exiled. Pope seems half to
see this himself and snatches an aside:

> (Beasts, urg'd by us, their Fellow Beasts pursue,
> And learn of Man each other to undo.)—

which is the explanation he gives for the savagery of the past, though he doesn't, naturally enough, try to explain exactly how pike, 'the Tyrants of the watry Plains', learned their ways.

But the difficulty lies at the very root of the poem, and it was to go on troubling his work to the end. Behind his acceptance of the ideas, the 'Augustan' philosophic order, according to which the world was in the end *harmoniously confused* and moral values, for all their apparent confusion, equally harmonious—'T'observe a Mean, be to himself a Friend,/To follow Nature, and regard his End'—lay a profound, uneasy, never-quite-acknowledged recognition that the world showed anything but the order a civilized mind required, and that to follow nature was not to 'observe a mean' but somehow to find, or create, one from among its stresses. In *Windsor Forest* he never faces the real difficulties of doing this. The youthful Poet sees his part as retirement from the world to the 'shades' of nature, with its 'charms' and 'humbler joys'. Consciously to keep one's distance is an easy way to see an ideal harmony in things.

It is the strength of *The Rape of the Lock*, of course, that Pope does not retire from heroes' wits and beaux' snuff-boxes, tweezer-cases, broken vows and death-bed alms,

> And Lover's Hearts with Ends of Riband bound;
> The Courtier's Promises, and Sick Man's Pray'rs,
> The Smiles of Harlots, and the Tears of Heirs,
> Cages for Gnats, and Chains to Yoak a Flea;
> Dry'd Butterflies, and Tomes of Casuistry.

But as this striking foreshadow of *The Dunciad* suggests, Pope does not get much below the surface of such things in *The Rape of the Lock*. Brilliant, subtle, engaging as it is, and probably the finest poem in the language by so young a man, it is after all the work of a man of only 26. Inevitably, he handles life with an airy, knowing allusiveness that has to serve for inner experience of it. When he evokes its beauty, for instance, he idealizes—

> Loose to the Wind their airy Garments flew,
> Thin glitt'ring Textures of the filmy Dew;
> Dipt in the richest Tincture of the Skies . . .

Even when he touches the vulgar he remains elegantly 'witty'— 'Maids turn'd Bottels, call aloud for Corks', and the like. The scintillations are light and quick, catching the uneven surface of a highly conscious society with an even sharper consciousness of the thoughtlessness and violence shaping the surface from within:

> . . . At ev'ry Word a Reputation dies.
> *Snuff*, or the *Fan*, supply each Pause of Chat,
> With singing, laughing, ogling, and all that.

Mean while, declining from the Noon of Day,
The Sun obliquely shoots his burning Ray;
The hungry Judges soon the Sentence sign,
And Wretches hang that Jury men may Dine;
The Merchants from th' *Exchange* returns in Peace,
And the long Labours of the *Toilette* cease ...

In its grasp of reality, a world ranging from gossip to the gallows, this is far richer than anything in *Windsor Forest*—richer indeed than almost anything since the early 17th century. And yet we need only put it beside some of Pope's later work—besides the epistle *Of the Characters of Women*, for example—in order to see how relatively simple are the juxtapositions and feelings of *The Rape of the Lock*. In fact, it too is concerned not so much with actual men and women, and how they really live or might live, as with the *idea* of Society. Pope's consciousness here assimilates the energy, the wit, the formal structure by which he explores the idea, but they are directed to that and of course limited by it.

II

After any of these early poems, the world of the first *Dunciad* seems at once more diverse, more lively, more fully adult. Pope's imagination moves easily from butchers to the fall of Rome, but it now sees the gross details of life more directly and draws greater strength from them as a result:

Like the vile straw that's blown about the streets
The needy Poet sticks to all he meets,
Coach'd, carted, trod upon, now loose, now fast,
In the Dog's tail his progress ends at last.

The result, flexible and assured as it is, hardly catches the crackling comic energy, the masterful pounce, of the later version. Pope cannot yet produce verse of the order of—

Swearing and supperless the Hero sate,
Blasphem'd his Gods, the Dice, and damn'd his Fate,
Then gnaw'd his pen, then dash'd it on the ground,
Sinking from thought to thought, a vast profound!
Plung'd for his sense, but found no bottom there,
Yet wrote and flounder'd on, in mere despair.
Round him much Embryo, much Abortion lay,
Much future Ode, and abdicated Play;
Nonsense precipitate, like running Lead,
That slip'd thro' Cracks and Zig-zags of the Head;

All that on Folly Frenzy could beget,
Fruits of dull Heat, and Sooterkins of Wit.
Next, o'er his Books his eyes began to roll,
In pleasing memory of all he stole,
How here he sipp'd, how there he plunder'd snug
And suck'd all o'er, like an industrious Bug.

Nevertheless, even in the first version Pope's consciousness of himself seems to have become more absorbed into the consciousness of a denser, more varied reality. In so far as he is aware of himself, he sees clearly enough the importance of his own 'wit' in the poem and of its power to evoke a 'sense' beyond the grasp of the Dunces. Nor is it any coincidence that his best verse could well be described in his own phrases: 'Wit's wild, dancing light' (illuminating the 'native night' of Dullness), 'Elasticity and Fire', and so on. He is in fact not less, but more perfectly conscious of himself as a poet, better able to understand his own activity and to use that understanding in wider judgment, without losing imaginative spontaneity.

On the other hand, it is by no means a complete understanding, as the rather inert structure betrays. When we try to see the poem as a whole, it is hard not to conclude that the mock-heroic framework (together with the others that have been found in it—the Lord Mayor's procession, etc.) meant more to Pope than he manages to make it mean to the reader. It hardly irradiates the work. It provides him with opportunities for a series of raids, but whatever strategic effect he intended by them, the results tend to lack any essential coherence. Such form as the poem has at its best (the passages above are cases in point) does not lie in any contrast, felt continuously and in detail, between sordid reality on the one hand and Heroic, Aristocratic, or Christian-humanist values on the other. What flashes out of the poetry is an imaginative structure not properly visible until the later version. As in the passages above, the world he perceives is judged in, and by, the perceiving; and the poetic form lies not in an externally conceived patterning of Values, but rather in the complex, apprehending wit: the evident vitality with which he catches potential vitality running meaninglessly to waste, away from human consciousness into grossness or vulgarity or grotesque blown straw: ultimately, to 'precipitate nonsense', 'frenzy', 'industrious bugs'.

This is much more evident in the revisions and certainly in Book IV, where the formal framework matters even less. Such as it is, the 'structure' there is quite external to the real 'order' and 'light' of the poetry and to Pope's deeply animating sense of chaos, night, and death—

> Ye Pow'rs! whose Mysteries restor'd I sing,
> To whom Time bears me on his rapid wing,

Suspend a while your Force inertly strong,
Then take at once the Poet and the Song.

These are structured on his comic recognition that the song cele-
brating the triumphs of Chaos represents a victory against it. As in
the lines Leavis has discussed—'First slave to Words, then vassal to
a Name...'—where the verse embodies the insights and judgments
whose absence they describe, so in the re-imagined ending of the
poem (from the yawn onwards). As a comparison with its first version
shows very clearly, its greatness lies in the power with which Pope
evokes the opposing power of inertia and chaos, the complete mastery
of his ordering energy over the disordering forces he evokes, and his
complete awareness of this and why it matters, all of which make the
final vision, for example, both a comically exaggerated fantasy and a
menacing reality at the same time. That the first version relies so
heavily on its formal contrasts nevertheless, only illustrates how much,
ten years or so after his early poems, he still felt the need of an acceptable form for his poetic energy, one able to contain his 'wit' and also
give it public significance, and yet how difficult it was to find one
among the conventions and attitudes at hand.

The strain was harder to avoid the more consciously Pope saw
himself as the poet-sage of his time. 'Augustanism', we might remember (like the beliefs lumped together as 'the Elizabethan world-
picture', or similar handy constructs), embraces only the ideas, feelings and judgments the finest minds of the age shared with the
fifth-rate ones. Genuine artists do not merely reflect, they also create,
the consciousness of their age. The possibilities and order they discover as 'life' are not simply the 'facts' and order their age most firmly
believes in—or thinks it ought to believe in. Pope was no exception,
I think, despite his own imperfect consciousness of the point, and despite the tendency of critics and historians since to treat him as almost
the official expositor of 'Augustan' ideals that he sometimes tried
to be. Pope in that role, with that conception of his art, is generally
Pope at his weakest.

The *Essay on Man* makes clear enough how bad he could be as a
philosopher. Johnson's strictures—especially from the man who
answered Soames Jenyn—are unanswerable: 'Never was penury of
knowledge and vulgarity of sentiment so happily disguised'. On the
other hand, as the obvious similarities between *Epistle IV*, for instance, and *The Vanity of Human Wishes* may remind us, it is not
all empty or banal. As Johnson half saw, Pope's trouble was not just
philosophical incompetence. If most of his ideas are unconvincing,
they also tend to lack imaginative conviction. There is, as Brower
for one has pointed out, a 'strain between *philosophy* and *sensibility*',
all through Pope's philosophical poems, but I think it runs much

deeper and means more than Brower suggests. For the strain seems to lie between Pope's desire (almost *will*) to believe in an ideal, universal, transcendent Order, which all men should serve, and the far richer, more spontaneous vitality with which he cannot help but respond to, the vitality of the actual, contradictory, myriad, unordered world around him.

The famous opening of *Epistle II* illustrates this at a crucial point in his argument—where he turns to *explain*, as best he can, what he always most deeply felt: how life is both created and destroyed by its own anarchic energies. 'Presume not God to scan', he begins, and yet he immediately avoids doing so himself only by refusing to recognize what his lines imply. The passive voice—'plac'd on this isthmus...' 'created half to rise...'—certainly puts the emphasis on man; the active 'placing' and 'creating' are suggested nevertheless, and they strike curious overtones when the issue of final ends emerges. For what seems at first sight only a commonplace—'Born but to die, and reas'ning but to err'—looks rather different when its ambiguous syntax is echoed a few lines later in 'Created half to rise, and half to fall'. By that point, indeed, the impetus of the lines seems to have carried Pope into deeper waters; an underside of doubt and terror peeps through the lofty detachment:

> Created half to rise, *and half to fall*;
> Great lord of all things, *yet a prey to all*;
> Sole judge of Truth, in endless Error *hurl'd*:
> The glory, jest, and riddle of the world!

The stress falls on man as a helpless victim. By this point, the isthmus has come to seem so narrow, the violence so great, the frustration so complete, that man's 'glory', when Pope triumphantly asserts it, almost seems to consist in surviving such overpowering and malignant 'jests'.

There are other signs, of course: the somewhat bullying exclamations with which Pope tries to ram home some of his conclusions ('Presumptuous man!' ... 'Vile worm!' ... 'Thou fool!' ... and so forth); the confusions, age-old no doubt, but glaringly obvious here, about Reason's ability to guide the Passions it gives 'edge and pow'r' to, or the benevolence of nature that feeds on destruction, or the value of an Eternal Art that amuses itself by creating illusionary 'baubles' to keep us happily bemused. All through the poem, in fact, we find a difference between the animated, concrete way Pope responds to the extremes, the varied (almost absurdly varied) possibilities of life, and the flatly assertive way he propounds its supposed metaphysical order: 'Die of a rose in aromatic pain'—'All Nature is but Art, unknown to thee'. As Brower has suggested, Pope's conception of his task is curious indeed:

> Laugh where we must, be candid where we can;
> But vindicate the ways of God to Man;

and the more we ponder the poetry of the *Essay*, the more significant that 'but' seems.

Various critics have noted that he runs into similar difficulties in the *Moral Essays* associated with the *Essay on Man*. The doctrine of the Ruling Passion is only the most notorious case, where his attempt to show a philosophical 'order' is clearly inept. There is also the philosophizing about 'sense' in the 4th *Essay*—certainly not inept, but not as sharply felt as Timon's lack of 'sense' or the over-whelming fertility of 'laughing Ceres': even the conclusion, noble as it is, envisages an ideal order of human and natural life with a response, a 'force and life' (to use Leavis's phrase) noticeably less concrete. (The obvious comparison with Jonson's 'To Penshurst' is not alto-gether in Pope's favour.) It is also easy to see why Pope laboured so long with the more complex and finer *Essay III, Of the Use of Riches*. All through it he clearly feels the immense impersonal *power* of money; his difficulty is to know what to think of it. In theory he does know: the desire to get or to spend it perverts natural and human good; and for the most part his indictment of a capitalist society has a tremendous force. But how can a man avoid the power of money when he lives in a society built upon it? No one can remain indifferent, as Pope himself knew. Here, he argues on the one hand that the desire to possess it and the desire to dissipate it are equally 'natural' and therefore 'good':

> Hear then the truth: "Tis Heav'n each Passion sends,
> And diff'rent men directs to diff'rent ends.
> Extremes in Nature equal good produce,
> Extremes in Man concur to gen'ral use.'
> Ask we what makes one keep, and one bestow?
> That POW'R who bids the Ocean ebb and flow,
> Bids seed-time, harvest, equal course maintain,
> Thro' reconcil'd extremes of drought and rain,
> Builds Life on Death, on Change Duration founds,
> And gives th'·eternal wheels to know their rounds.

> Riches, like insects, when conceal'd they lie,
> Wait but for wings, and in their season, fly.
> Who sees pale Mammon pine amidst his store,
> Sees but a backward steward for the Poor;
> This year a Reservoir, to keep and spare,
> The next, a Fountain, spouting thro' his Heir,
> In lavish streams to quench a Country's thirst,
> And men and dogs shall drink him 'till they burst.

This is indeed 'religious in its seriousness', but is it all equally serious? No amount of exegesis, I think, can alter the difference between the profound sense of life imagined in those far-reaching, paradoxical 'extremes', and the rather notional claim for their 'equal good'. Water remains water indeed; but we hardly need the account of Cotta and his son that immediately follows this passage to wonder how far Pope really *saw* the extremes as 'reconcil'd'. Whatever happens must, somehow, be for the best, even though greed withholds the water so long and folly dispenses it so lavishly that thirsty men and dogs drink it 'till they burst'. The absurdly diverse extremes are imagined more solidly, more vividly, than the reconciling benevolence of Heaven.

However, Pope also tries to define a morality of *balance*: 'That secret rare, between th'extremes to move/Of mad Good-nature, and of mean Self-love'. Leaving aside the philosophical relations between this and the ends Heaven has in mind, we may still remain unconvinced by the 'balanced' Man of Ross—in whom Pope portrays what he thinks he means by an ideal human vitality, yet portrays it with a singular lack of it himself.

> Whose Cause-way parts the vale with shady rows?
> Whose Seats the weary Traveller repose?
> Who taught that heav'n-directed spire to rise?
> THE MAN OF ROSS, each lisping babe replies . . .

The only thing sharply realized in the whole passage seems to be, not the Man of Ross's 'clear and artless' use of the 'waters' of life, but his actual income: 'five hundred pounds a year'. In fact, however, vital 'balance' in Pope means something less flimsy than the Man of Ross passage, less withdrawn from the realities of the world. It is embodied in the account of Cotta and his son, or Villiers and Cutler, where his wide-ranging imagination seizes life in its oddity, disorder, strife, extremes, with an answering (but morally questioning) vivacity that actively creates and embodies a 'balance':

> In the worst inn's worst room, with mat half-hung,
> The floors of plaister, and the walls of dung,
> On once a flock-bed, but repair'd with straw,
> With tape-ty'd curtains, never meant to draw,
> The George and Garter dangling from that bed
> Where tawdry yellow strove with dirty red,
> Great Villiers lies—alas! how chang'd from him,
> That life of pleasure, and that soul of whim!

The judgment implied in the Virgilian-Miltonic reference, for example, is fused with the actuality of the bed: this is not hell, nor are we out of it. Perhaps Pope himself was conscious of a difference between the Man of Ross passage and this; the way he ends the poem,

with the superbly sharp and lively account of Sir Balaam, suggests
he was.

III

In the Preface to his volume of 1717, Pope observed that 'the life
of a Wit is a warfare upon earth', and the epigram makes an apt comment
on his own best work, though in a more complex sense than he
could have meant when he made it. The highest life of his wit is certainly
a warfare, not only directed *at* the earth he inhabited, but also
an inextricable part of it. At his greatest, he does not simply oppose
clear-cut doctrines or principles against an imperfect world, but participates
in the endless conflicts that make it imperfect. Nor does he
trust simply in the formulas or accepted ideals of his society, but
rather seeks whatever values emerge in his balancing realization of the
conflicting elements. He is less conscious of a known, integral 'self'
confronting a perplexing or inimical 'reality', than of a more fluid,
unknown self to be discovered within the perplexities and oppositions.
His finest consciousness, therefore, is not so much the moralist's rectitude,
'the strong Antipathy of Good to Bad', as the kind embodied
in the whole *Epistle to Dr Arbuthnot* for example, where the image
of himself as moralist is only one stroke in a larger imaginative composition.
This more inclusive, more subtle, and more relaxed sense
of his own life as a Wit accompanies a similarly more mature sense of
life around him. Thus the end of his *Imitation* of Horace's *Epistles*,
I, i (addressed to Bolingbroke) forms a highly relevant comment
on the *Essay on Man*. Pope takes the Horatian opportunity
wholeheartedly:

> You laugh, half Beau half Sloven if I stand,
> My Wig all powder, and all snuff my Band;
> You laugh, if Coat and Breeches strangely vary,
> White Gloves, and Linnen worthy Lady Mary!
> But when no Prelate's Lawn with Hair-shirt lin'd,
> Is half so incoherent as my Mind,
> When (each Opinion with the next at strife,
> One ebb and flow of follies all my Life)
> I plant, root up, I build, and then confound,
> Turn round to square, and square again to round;
> You never change one muscle of your face ...

The echo of the *Essay* a few lines later points the difference. Pope's
awareness of Man's absurdity now includes an awareness of his own
—even as a philosopher trying to conquer it. What is more, the
awareness is now a part of his everyday perception, not reserved for

special philosophical occasions; it is more keenly specific, more alive to the actual striving elements in which life consists. Although (prompted by Horace) he now recognizes their final irreconcilability far more clearly than in the *Essay*, he neither tries to argue the facts into a tidy system nor grows pompous about them. By creating a social intimacy so easy and yet so finely measured, and involving us in it too, he also makes us see that the way he recognizes the facts, his tone, his sense of a possible human civility, is as important as the facts themselves.

This is the general strategy of the *Epistle to Dr Arbuthnot* of course. Firmly placing us at once with him on the inside of his door, Pope evokes not only the silliness of society 'outside'—brilliantly focused in its attitude to a famous poet—but also the genuine society 'within' —again brilliantly focused in Pope's heartfelt but humorously self-aware exasperation with the fools.

> No place is sacred, not the Church is free,
> Ev'n *Sunday* shines no *Sabbath-day* to me:
> Then from the *Mint* walks forth the Man of Ryme,
> Happy! to catch me, just at Dinner-time.
>   Is there a Parson, much be-mus'd in Beer,
> A maudlin Poetess, a ryming Peer,
> A Clerk, foredoom'd his Father's soul to cross,
> Who pens a Stanza when he should *engross*? . . .
> All fly to *Twit'nam* . . .

We cannot but share his feelings; and as he gradually develops them he gradually articulates the social and moral values they imply. Indeed, he manipulates his 'persona' so shrewdly that we almost smile as we respond to its essential truth.

Yet even so palpable a design on us does not make us admire either the poem or Pope any the less. The self-awareness is real *within* the design; easily, with perfect control, Pope realizes what he is doing and what his doing it represents. He now sees his world with all its confusions implicated in one another, and sees his feelings—of delight, scorn, sympathy, bitterness, moral fervour, and so on—to be correspondingly implicated.

> Amphibious Thing! that acting either Part,
> The trifling Head, or the corrupted Heart!
> Fop at the Toilet, Flatt'rer at the Board,
> Now trips a Lady, and now struts a Lord.
> *Eve*'s Tempter thus the Rabbins have exprest,
> A Cherub's face, a Reptile all the rest;
> Beauty that shocks you, Parts that none will trust,
> Wit that can creep, and Pride that licks the dust.

D

> Not Fortune's Worshipper, nor Fashion's Fool,
> Not Lucre's Madman, nor Ambition's Tool,
> Not proud, nor servile, be one Poet's praise
> That, if he pleas'd, he pleas'd by manly ways;
> That Flatt'ry, ev'n to Kings, he held a shame,
> And thought a Lye in Verse or Prose the same. . . .

The disruptive force of the antithesis *becomes* the cohesive force of
the moral centre ('the same'); the mind discovers itself—its social
and moral values, and also its separateness—at the centre where all
its critical responses to the diverse phenomena of life are balanced.
The weakest part of the poem, significantly, is the ending, where Pope
tries to formulate his ideals directly, and in effect *reduces* them to
a conscious simplicity. To place the last 30 or 40 lines against the
first is to see how much his poetic vitality depends on the very 'Strife',
even the 'Pride' and 'Rage', he tries to dismiss in the ending.

If, however, our social being is fine, the full scope of human nature
is finer, and of course it is no part of *Arbuthnot* to consider its grander
or more tragic possibilities. When Pope did try to do so, his difficulty
was to avoid his conscious ideas getting in the way—though naturally
he never saw it like that himself. A passage like the ending of the
Epilogue to the Satires I, for example, succeeds because its prophetic
vision is also a social act:

> Lo! at the Wheels of her Triumphal Car,
> Old *England*'s Genius, rough with many a Scar,
> Dragg'd in the Dust! his Arms hang idly round,
> His Flag inverted trails along the ground!
> Our Youth, all liv'ry'd o'er with foreign Gold,
> Before her dance; behind her crawl the Old!
> See thronging Millions to the Pagod run,
> And offer Country, Parent, Wife, or Son!
> Hear her black Trumpet thro' the Land proclaim,
> That 'Not to be corrupted is the Shame.'
> In Soldier, Churchman, Patriot, Man in Pow'r,
> 'Tis Avarice all, Ambition is no more!
> See, all our Nobles begging to be Slaves!
> See, all our Fools aspiring to be Knaves!
> The Wit of Cheats, the Courage of a Whore,
> Are what ten thousand envy and adore.
> All, all look up, with reverential Awe,
> On Crimes that scape, or triumph o'er the Law:
> While Truth, Worth, Wisdom, daily they decry—
> 'Nothing is Sacred now but Villany.'
>
> Yet may this Verse (if such a Verse remain)
> Show there was one who held it in disdain.

The end of Book IV of *The Dunciad* is another obvious case. Such passages carry a kind of religious horror, a realization that men can, and do, not just practise villainy but actually worship it. The social reality, felt in specific and telling detail, the moral judgments elicited from within its particulars as they are apprehended, the darker possibilities seen pressing themselves forward, the visionary grandeur, and the assured self-consciousness that can, for example, manage so easily the shift of tone at the end of the passage just quoted: all these somehow fuse together in a spontaneous act that reveals the significance both of what is seen and also of seeing it in that way.

Nevertheless, in talking about Pope's very greatest poetry, it is obviously misleading to leave the emphasis on visionary grandeur: for one thing, that is not its characteristic note, and for another, its power is more flexible. It is better represented, I think, in parts of the *Moral Essays,* especially of the second and third. The 'philosophic' generalizations about women in the former are not very impressive—they sound, indeed, all too like club-table cant: 'the Love of Pleasure, and the Love of Sway' and so forth. The end of the poem, however, is very much more alive to the 'contradictions' of its subject. Pope can envisage even an ideal human character only as a 'blend ..., in exception to all gen'ral rules', of contradictory qualities. As the abstractions line up—Reserve with Frankness, Art and Truth, Courage and Softness, Modesty and Pride, 'Fix'd Principles' and 'Fancy ever new' —they seem more and more impossible, even to Pope; as with the earlier and slighter Epistle ('After the Coronation'), he recognizes the fact in a half-humorous gallantry: Heaven 'shakes all together, and produces—You'. He also recognizes the implication for himself: his role as a poet is to realize the ideal possibilities of human life in perhaps the only way they can be fully realized on earth—'The gen'rous God, who Wit and Gold refines .../To You gave Sense, Goodhumour, and a Poet'. The pivotal lines come just before all this; and their intensely sharp, deeply moving power, outstanding as it is here, seem to me of a piece with Pope's whole *oeuvre* : typical of him and of him alone.

> Pleasures the sex, as children Birds, pursue,
> Still out of reach, yet never out of view,
> Sure, if they catch, to spoil the Toy at most,
> To covet flying, and regret when lost:
> At last, to follies Youth could scarce defend,
> It grows their Age's prudence to pretend;
> Asham'd to own they gave delight before,
> Reduc'd to feign it, when they give no more:
> As Hags hold Sabbaths, less for joy than spight,
> So these their merry, miserable Night;

> Still round and round the Ghosts of Beauty glide,
> And haunt the places where their Honour dy'd.
>   See how the World its Veterans rewards!
> A Youth of frolicks, an old Age of Cards,
> Fair to no purpose, artful to no end,
> Young without Lovers, old without a Friend,
> A Fop their Passion, but their Prize a Sot,
> Alive, ridiculous, and dead, forgot!

As Empson says, in his analysis of some of these lines, they compel by their mixture of 'finicking precision' on the one hand, and on the other (what gives the almost comic 'finicking' quality its strength) their 'pity, bitterness and terror ... feelings ... of waste, of unavoidable futility'. Pope's vision, reaching beyond the characters of women to the very nature of things, is firmly centred on his social milieu and the tragic depths of life at the same time. And although Empson does not discuss the paradoxes in the first and third lines of the second paragraph, they are clearly essential. So too is the naturalness with which Pope can use the metaphor of 'Veterans'. The insight it involves is now an organic part of his consciousness, so that while his verse knowingly embodies a social life contrasting with the social reality, serves 'the World' in a very different sense, it creates it out of a savage, almost brooding, awareness of the waste and destruction it itself triumphs over.

Like this passage, the end of the third *Moral Essay*, the tale of Sir Balaam, seems to me one of the great touchstones in literature. It is very much more than a comment on the pervasive money-values of the age. The way Pope introduces it, for example, suggests that he at last recognized the vanity of dogmatizing as he turned to the possible religious sanctions for human conduct on earth. Nor is the reference to Job merely a device. The fate of the London merchant, who has greatness almost thrust upon him by the Devil and the pressure of his own society, becomes both a comic inversion and a re-creation of the profoundly disturbing questioning of Job's. For there is no mistaking how much life Pope sees in the society he is attacking, how much its detail animates his own dominating touch, his own quick, sure, vivid, wonderful creative comic energy—

> 'Live like yourself,' was soon my Lady's word;
> And lo! two puddings smoak'd upon the board.

> .   .   .

> 'Till all the Daemon makes his full descent,
> In one abundant show'r of Cent. per Cent.

> .   .   .

> My Lady falls to play; so bad her chance,
> He must repair it; takes a bribe from France;
> The House impeach him; Coningsby harangues;
> The Court forsake him, and Sir Balaam hangs;
> Wife, son, and daughter, Satan, are thy own,
> His wealth, yet dearer, forfeit to the Crown:
> The Devil and the King divide the prize,
> And sad Sir Balaam curses God and dies.

Sir Balaam is never simply the object of Pope's disengaged criticism. If he is a pitiful victim of the Devil, the poetry also makes us ask where the Devil gets *his* power: the vivacity is sharpened by the hint of a possible terror as well. Ultimately, Pope makes us see Sir Balaam as both the representative and the victim of forces in which we are all implicated whether we will or not. Once again (the last line only crystallizes the effect) he reaches through social life ('Things change their titles, as our manners turn') to the baffling foundations of human life. In some ways the whole passage recalls Jonson's Volpone or Sir Epicure Mammon; in fact, the writing is not only funnier, but far deeper, tougher, more densely and searchingly alive than Jonson's. The same is equally true if we think of Dickens or George Eliot instead, for those comparisons come readily to mind too. Like much else in Pope, if perhaps more obviously than most of his work, this passage reveals how much he concentrates many of the creative strengths of 17th-century poetry and at the same time—in ways that Defoe, for example, does not—look forward to the great 19th-century novelists. He created for his age, and in another sense for ours as well, what Henry James, writing on the first day of our century, 'hungered and thirsted' for: 'a gleam of reflection of the life *we* live, of artistic or plastic intelligence of it, something one can say yes or no to, as discrimination, perception, observation, rendering. . . .' But that life and that artistic intelligence of it gleam most brightly as they also reflect the 'chaos' and 'darkness' that paradoxically sustain them.

From 'Alexander Pope', in the *Melbourne Critical Review*, no. 7, 1964, pp. 49–65.

J. M. CAMERON

Pope's Use of 'Nature'

... TILLOTSON, [in *Pope and Human Nature*] has taken on a formid-able job in attempting to give an account of Pope's use of certain concepts. I shall confine myself to what he has to say about Pope's use of 'nature'; and I shall try to show that what he has to say will not do, either as an account of the concept which Pope received or as an account of Pope's use of the concept; and here I shall confine myself to one work, the *Essay on Criticism*.

Tillotson distinguishes two senses of 'nature'. First, there is 'Nature' defined as follows:

'I am aware of Pope as a poet who subscribed to the old belief that poets put as much human nature as possible into their poems, that they look to mankind—or Nature, as it was called in Pope's day—for their theme. . . . Nature, when it was not human hands and feet, was, and of course is still, that quantum of the mind-and-heart which all men —past, present, and in theory future—hold in common.'[1]

This is not very much like a definition, but Tillotson himself says he has in the passage I have quoted 'defined' the sense in which he is going to use 'Nature'. Another sense of 'nature' is intended when the capital letter is omitted: this is 'nature' as meaning 'merely the material universe'.[2] Later, Tillotson glances at the history of the term,[3] referring to Aristotle, Cicero, St Vincent of Lerins (at a further stage of the book he even slides into treating the *quod ubique, quod semper, quod ab omnibus* of St Vincent as 'St Vincent's definition of Nature'[4]), Quintilian, Longinus, Shakespeare, Dryden, Milton, Dave-nant, Hobbes, Wordsworth, Johnson, Tennyson, Thackeray, Arnold, George Eliot, Charles Reade and Voltaire. All these writers could certainly with propriety be cited in a history of the concept of nature. What is somewhat puzzling and even alarming is that Tillotson seems

---

[1] *Pope and Human Nature*, p. 1.   [3] *Ibid.*, pp. 19 ff.
[2] *Ibid.*, p. v.   [4] *Ibid.*, p. 72.

to imply that in all these cases 'nature' has a roughly similar connotation; equally puzzling and equally alarming, if we were really concerned with the history of the concept, is the omission of any reference to the three writers (in English) whose discussions of the concept are really decisive: Hooker, Locke and Hume. But in fact we are not at all concerned with the history of the concept. If we really were concerned with the history of the concept we should have to bring out that Aristotle's *physis*, for example, is not at all the same concept as Hobbes's 'nature' and entails a different and contradictory set of logical consequences. All that Tillotson wishes to say is that the literature which common consent places in the canon is concerned with the exploration and statement of what is common to men considered as desiring and passionate, feeling, and rational animals—he quotes, and this is the heart of his contention, Arnold's tag about 'the great primary human affections' which are the subject-matter of great literature. That this is often what writers have meant when they have made use of 'nature' as a critical criterion is true; but it is profoundly unilluminating as a comment upon the history of the concept from Aristotle to the nineteenth century; and, as I shall show, it is inadequate as a help to the analysis of Pope's use of the concept.

I shall now examine the *Essay on Criticism*, with the *Essay on Man*[5] perhaps the most 'philosophical' of Pope's works, in order to establish two points: that Pope is not relying upon the concept of nature as defined by Tillotson; and that Pope *uses* the ambiguities of the concept—ambiguities which arise out of its complex history—in order to frame, not a critical *argument*[6] in any way to be compared with the critical work of Aristotle or Johnson or Coleridge, but a poem capable of evoking an attitude to criticism and to the subject-matter of criticism.

In so far as we attempt to analyse the *Essay* into its component critical doctrines and arguments, it turns out to be a mosaic of scraps from Aristotle, Horace, Boileau and other critics. An early passage appears to contain advice on the practice of criticism.

> First follow Nature, and your judgment frame
> By her just standard, which is still the same:

[5] I have discussed the *Essay on Man* in 'Doctrinal to an Age: Notes towards a Revaluation of Pope's *Essay on Man*', *Dublin Review*, Second Quarter 1951, No. 452.

[6] Professor Sutherland seems to me profoundly wrong (about Pope, not perhaps about Dryden) where he writes: 'The poetry of Dryden, Pope, Thomson, Johnson, Gray, Goldsmith is not *merely* a poetry of good sense, but good sense it is. The poetical structure is not held together by emotional stresses but by a sort of *steel framework of intellectual argument*.' (My italics.) James Sutherland, *A Preface to Eighteenth Century Poetry*, 1948, p. 161. I may add that this is one of the few places where I would venture to disagree with Professor Sutherland.

> Unerring NATURE, still divinely bright,
> One clear, unchanged, and universal light,
> Life, force, and beauty, must to all impart,
> At once the source, and end, and test of Art.
> Art from that fund each just supply provides;
> Works without show, and without pomp presides:
> In some fair body thus th' informing soul
> With spirits feeds, with vigor fills the whole,
> Each motion guides, and ev'ry nerve sustains;
> Itself unseen, but in th' effects remains.

(ll. 68–79)

Plainly these lines contain no useful advice: they express, with great vigour and precision, an *attitude*; and it would be a mistake to ask in too peremptory a voice: What does it mean? i.e. What propositions expressible in other words can be squeezed out of the passage? It is precisely as the expression of an attitude to poetry and the criticism of poetry that the *Essay is impressive*, both as illustrating, in action as it were, Pope's sensibility and intelligence, and as illuminating the valuations of the literary society of which Pope was so self-conscious a member.[7]

> 'Tis hard to say, if greater want of skill
> Appear in writing or in judging ill;
> But, of the two, less dang'rous is th' offence
> To tire our patience, than mislead our sense.
> Some few in that, but numbers err in this,
> Ten censure wrong for one who writes amiss;
> A fool might once himself alone expose,
> Now one in verse makes many more in prose.
>
> 'Tis with our judgments as our watches, none
> Go just alike, yet each believes his own.
> In Poets as true Genius is but rare,
> True Taste as seldom is the Critic's share;
> Both must alike from Heav'n derive their light,
> These born to judge, as well as those to write.
> Let such teach others who themselves excel,
> And censure freely who have written well.
> Authors are partial to their wit, 'tis true,
> But are not Critics to their judgment, too?

[7] Tillotson makes an excellent point when he observes: '[Pope's] unfolding of a poet's personality is a new thing in English poetry, being completer than that of Donne, who from this point of view is his strongest predecessor.' *Pope and Human Nature*, p. 142.

Yet if we look more closely, we shall find
Most have the seeds of judgment in their mind:
Nature affords at least a glimm'ring light;
The lines, tho' touch'd but faintly, are drawn right.
But as the slightest sketch, if justly trac'd,
Is by ill-colouring but the more disgrac'd,
So by false learning is good sense defac'd:
Some are bewilder'd in the maze of schools,
And some made coxcombs Nature meant but fools.
In search of wit these lose their common sense,
And then turn Critics in their own defence:
Each burns alike, who can, or cannot write,
Or with a Rival's, or an Eunuch's spite.
All fools have still an itching to deride,
And fain would be upon the laughing side.
If Maevius scribble in Apollo's spight,
There are, who judge still worse than he can write.

(ll. 1–35)

We are given first a picture of the poet identifying himself with all
reasonable men (*'our* patience . . . *our* sense'), surrounded by a horde
of, in the main, foolish critics. They are perhaps more than foolish.
They may be *dangerous* (l. 3), even if they are also, and this is stressed
in the lines immediately following, obscenely ludicrous.

Some have at first for Wits, then Poets past,
Turn'd critics next, and prov'd plain fools at last.
Some neither can for Wits nor Critics pass,
As heavy mules are neither horse nor ass.
Those half-learn'd witlings, numerous in our isle,
As half-form'd insects on the banks of Nile;
Unfinish'd things, one knows not what to call,
Their generation's so equivocal:
To tell 'em would an hundred tongues require,
Or one vain wit's, that might a hundred tire.

(ll. 36–45)

The 'Tis hard to say' of the beginning is designed to give an impression of fair-mindedness; but with the arrival of the images of the mule
and the abortive insects we know that the poet is taking sides, though
the initial assumption of fairness and Olympian detachment somehow
persuades us that he has a right to bestow praise and blame.

Next: original endowment is not a matter of skill, at least, not of
our skill. The comparison between 'judgments' and 'watches' (this
figure has an ancestry and a posterity) suggests that 'Heaven's' skill is
in question, that is, the rules by which human nature has been framed

are a *techne* analogous to the art of making clockwork mechanisms.[8]
Both the critic and the poet are the creatures of Heaven; and this
carries with it the implication that Pope is exploring, and describing
in an authoritative way, a providential order; but the whole tone is
that of one who surveys the scene rather than that of one who participates in it.

Nature provides for all. But what a botch most make of this provision! No doubt 'Most have the seeds of judgement in their mind';
but the impression Pope conveys is of a swarming multitude of malignant fools.

By l.45 Pope has thus created the impression—though this is not
what he explicitly *says*—that the true critic, even one who is potentially such, is a rare creature who, no matter how rich his natural
endowments, may more easily go wrong than not. There is thus a
deliberately created tension between Nature's provision, the providential order expounded with authority by Pope, and the presence
everywhere of human perversity. This dramatic tension is commended
to us by the double attitude expressed: on the one hand, the poet is,
like the rest of us, painstakingly peering through the gloom of a teas-
ingly difficult subject, on the other, he has an Olympian, god-like
power of surveying the scene with a penetrating gaze and estimating
the capacities and performances of the actors. This is calculated both
to reassure us—after all, he is one of us, he has his difficulties too—
and impress us—he speaks with authority. And we are disposed
(so far as we submit to the mood evoked by the poem) to accept the
authority precisely because it seems initially not to be claimed.

The vehicle of the argument is a diagram rather than a picture.
The poet of genius is represented as surrounded by a swarm of abor-
tions and monstrosities, the bad critics, those who have choked in
themselves 'the seeds of judgement'. And in spite of its being plainly
suggested that the endowments of the poet and the critic are different,
the large assumption is made, and enforced upon us by the very fact
that this is a poem, that the poet is here competent to establish the
rationale, the limitations and the methods of criticism.

An attitude having been established, a mood induced, Pope now
advances to an elaborate disquisition on 'nature', and this occupies the
remainder of the first part of the *Essay*.

'Nature' and 'the natural' are among the trickiest of concepts and
if Pope were concerned with anything at all resembling a philosophical
analysis and account, his first task would be to analyse what is in fact
a large and unruly family of concepts into its individual members, lest

[8] This idea is worked out in Hobbes's Introduction to *Leviathan*. 'Nature'
is here 'Art' in the sense of a *techne*, to be understood in the light of the
mechanical arts. Nothing could be farther from the Aristotelian *physis*, with
its emphasis on the analogy of organism.

the discussion should founder upon the ambiguities of the concepts. 'Natural', for example, can mean 'primitive', 'normal', 'right', 'good', 'uncivilized', 'civilized', 'factual', 'existing', and so on. It is pointless to ask what the *real* meaning of the term is: all these meanings are perfectly good since they all represent established uses. Now, Pope's procedure is the direct opposite of the philosophical. He *uses* the ambiguity of the concept, its being capable of suggesting a vast unruly family, to achieve a certain result.

Lines 68–79 have already been quoted. The poem continues:

> Some, to whom Heav'n in wit has been profuse,
> Want as much more to turn it to its use;
> For wit and judgment often are at strife,
> Tho' meant each other's aid, like man and wife.
> 'Tis more to guide, than spur the Muse's steed;
> Restrain his fury, than provoke his speed;
> The winged courser, like a gen'rous horse,
> Shews most true mettle when you check his course.
>
> Those RULES of old discover'd, not devis'd,
> Are Nature still, but Nature methodiz'd;
> Nature, like Liberty, is but restrain'd
> By the same Laws which first herself ordain'd.
>
> Hear how learn'd Greece her useful rules indites,
> When to repress, and when indulge our flights:
> High on Parnassus' top her sons she show'd,
> And pointed out those arduous paths they trod;
> Held from afar, aloft, th' immortal prize,
> And urg'd the rest by equal steps to rise.
> Just precepts thus from great example giv'n,
> She drew from them what they deriv'd from Heav'n.
>
> (ll. 80–99)

These senses of 'nature' may be distinguished. (1) A quasi-deity, infallible, unchanging, illuminating in virtue of its deity ('divinely bright'). (2) A source of power ('Life, force, and beauty'). (3) A repository of criteria for judgement ('your judgement frame/By her just standard'). (4) The *source* of art, perhaps as providing rules for a *techne*, certainly source as a fountain of energy, as the shaper—demiurge—of the world and men: through vagueness we can hold all these ideas as it were in solution. (5) The *end* of art; perhaps no more is suggested than that art has a purpose and that this purpose enjoys cosmic approval. (6) Nature *is* Art and Art *is* Nature; the two concepts are run together in lines 74–9. This is confirmed if we pass on to lines 88–91. Here it is said that the rules of art (to be summarily stated as: Don't let wit and judgement get out of balance—wit being roughly the original energy of the intellect, judgement the capacity to direct the original energy into particular channels) are 'Nature ... Nature methodiz'd'.

If we want to ask what kind of a noun, here, 'Nature' is, what it is used to represent, it is plain that there is more than one answer to the question. But this would surely be an inappropriate question. All the answers are necessary to Pope. In order to achieve the kind of effect he aims at Nature must simultaneously be God, the world, the soul of the world, the rules for the production of art, the standards of the critic, a reservoir of cosmic energy, the inspiration of the poet; even, as he begins to make clear at the end of the passage cited, and then goes on to elaborate, a particular body of literature, sometimes the work of one author, namely, Homer.

> When first young Maro in his boundless mind
> A work t' outlast immortal Rome design'd
> Perhaps he seem'd above the Critic's law,
> And but from Nature's fountain scorn'd to draw:
> But when t' examine ev'ry part he came,
> Nature and Homer were, he found, the same.
>
> (ll. 130–5)

An interesting specific use by Pope of one of the ambiguities is provided by the reference to the rules of ancient literature, especially Homer, as providing 'natural' guidance for the poet. This must cause difficulties and it is to be expected that Pope will provide himself with an escape-clause. Of course, he does so.

> Some beauties yet no Precepts can declare,
> For there's a happiness as well as care.
> Music resembles Poetry, in each
> Are nameless graces which no methods teach,
> And which a master-hand alone can reach.
> If, where the rules not far enough extend,
> (Since rules were made but to promote their end)
> Some lucky licence answer to the full
> Th' intent propos'd, that Licence is a rule.
> Thus Pegasus, a nearer way to take,
> May boldly deviate from the common track.
> Great wits sometimes may gloriously offend,
> And rise to faults true Critics dare not mend;
> From vulgar bounds with brave disorder part,
> And snatch a grace beyond the reach of art ...
>
> (ll. 141–55)

Now, the interest of this particular escape-clause is that it doesn't, as one might expect, rend the texture of the poem: for spontaneity, beauty uncovenanted for and uncontrived, that which is, as Pope perceives and states, analogous to Grace in the language of theology, are held within the general scope of the idea of Nature by the particular idea of Nature as a fountain of psychic energy; from such a fountain we should expect to draw spontaneity rather than rules. But the conflation of Nature as infinitely various and as predictably regular enables Pope to overcome what might otherwise be a destructive paradox.

In the last paragraph of the First Part—

> Still green with bays each ancient Altar stands
> Above the reach of sacrilegious hands

—Pope stresses the charm and prestige of classical culture under the image of the supernatural, though it is the supernatural domesticated by centuries of humanistic education in a Christian society. But with this ending, the disorderly junk-shop of concepts he has assembled—it is in fact a *résumé* of all those traditions in which the words *physis* and *natura* have had a role—is given an appearance of order and a sacred character. And Pope takes the opportunity to give himself a central place in the tradition, and to re-emphasize the combination of humility with authority he has imposed upon us at the beginning of the poem, in the closing lines of the First Part:

> Hail, Bards triumphant! born in happier days;
> Immortal heirs of universal praise!
> Whose honours with increase of ages grow,
> As streams roll down, enlarging as they flow;
> Nations unborn your mighty names shall sound,
> And worlds applaud that must not yet be found!
> O may some spark of your celestial fire,
> The last, the meanest of your sons inspire,
> (That on weak wings, from far, pursues your flights;
> Glows while he reads, but trembles as he writes)
> To teach vain Wits a science little known,
> T' admire superior sense, and doubt their own!
>
> (ll. 189–200)

Pope is 'the last, the meanest of your sons'; but he is a *son*, not an interloper in the family; and he prays to be a teacher, for it is he who is to instruct the 'vain Wits'.

With the Second Part of the *Essay* there is a change of tone and of atmosphere, and a conceptual change as well. One way of putting the change would be to say that there is a shift of level from the *cosmic* to the *moral*, from *natura naturans* and *natura naturata* to Nature as a compendium of the rules of prudence and morality. The shift is not complete; and it is interesting to note that in so far as Nature is still conceived as a creative force she has now a somewhat malign touch.

> Of all the causes which conspire to blind
> Man's erring judgement, and misguide the mind,
> What the weak head with strongest bias rules,
> Is *Pride*, the never-failing vice of fools.
> Whatever Nature has in worth deny'd,
> She gives in large recruits of needful Pride ...
>
>   (ll. 201–6)

This is to make Nature a fountain of stupidity.

I shall not offer a detailed analysis of the rest of the poem. My main purposes: to bring out the complexities and ambiguities of the concept of nature; to suggest that these complexities and ambiguities are rooted in the history of the concept; to show that the structure of the poem is not a 'steel framework of intellectual argument' but a wonderfully skilful exploitation of the conceptual ambiguities: have been accomplished by the analysis so far given.

We are now in a position to see the inadequacy of Tillotson's definitions and general account of 'nature'. He selects one use—that which is common to all men at all times—as central and primary, another—'the material universe', *natura naturata*—as the main secondary use; whereas it is clear from an examination of the *Essay on Criticism* alone that Pope's family of concepts is much richer and more various and that from the standpoint of poetic analysis, to say nothing of the history of ideas, Tillotson's account will not do. ...

From 'Mr Tillotson and Mr Pope', in *Dublin Review*, vol. 233, no. 480, 1959, pp. 153–70.

EDWARD NILES HOOKER

Pope on Wit:
The Essay on Criticism

...A CLOSE reading of the [*Essay on Criticism*] leaves no room for
doubting that Pope intended to convey what seemed to him the significant facts about the place of wit in literature, and that for some
reason it struck him as particularly desirable to do so. To understand
the *Essay*, therefore, we should address ourselves to three questions.
Why, in an essay devoted to the principles of criticism, does Pope
lavish space and attention on wit rather than on taste? Second, what
controversies being agitated at the time he was composing the poem
would have led Pope to take a stand, and how is that stand established
in the *Essay*? And third, what body of contemporary thought, more
or less parallel to his own, was available to him as he wrote, and how
can it illuminate the direction and implications of his thinking?

In the first place, Pope at the start, after describing the highest form
of artistic talent in the poet as true genius, and the highest gift of the
critic as true taste, proceeds to the principle that the best critics are
those who excel as authors (lines 15–16).[1] True taste, therefore, is best
revealed in the operations of genius. That genius and taste 'have so
intimate a Connection' is not an idea peculiar to Pope; as one of his
contemporaries remarked, 'there are Cases where they cannot be ...
separated, without almost taking away their Functions.[2] A discussion
of the art of criticism would be idle unless it expounded taste by revealing the ways and standards of genius.

Or, since genius is distressingly rare, one may, like Pope, examine
the ways of wit, that more inclusive thing, conceived of as literary talent
or as the distinguishing element in literature, the breath of life inform-
ing the dull clay. As Dryden had proclaimed, 'The composition of all

---

[1] References to and quotations from the *Essay on Criticism* are based on
George Sherburn's edition, *Selections from Pope* (New York: Nelson and
Sons, n.d.).

[2] Anon., *The Polite Arts* (1749), p. 15.

poems is, or ought to be, of wit. . . .'³ He meant, not ingenuity, but a
spark. The special gift of those who create literature is to 'invigorate
their conceptions, and strike Life into a whole Piece'; what would
otherwise remain leaden or sluggish is magically transformed by Flame
and Strength of Sense.⁴ Nothing could be more natural than that
Homer and Virgil, authors who possessed such qualities in the highest
degree, should be called 'these Two supreme Wits.'⁵ Fire, invention,
and imagination became inextricably associated with wit; they were
the life-giving forces—so David Abercromby meant when he said that
'we never write wittily, but when our Imagination is exalted to a certain degree of heat, destructive to our cold Dulness.'⁶ . . .
    Sense and judgment are the solid, useful stuff with which the writer
works, but wit is the magic that lifts the stuff to the plane of belle-
lettres. A critic must understand wit if he is to talk of literature. And
in an essay on literary criticism we should expect Pope to deal in
generous measure with the problem of wit.

But in 1711 there were additional reasons why he had to confront
the subject, reasons general and reasons personal. As for the general
reasons, no one at the time could have forgotten that outburst of hostili-
ties in 1698–1700, in which the righteous had beset the wits—and had
driven them to cover. It is true, of course, that the attack had been
directed overtly against specific forms of wit, the facetious varieties
which played with sex and trifled with religion and morality. But underneath lay an impulse more sinister, more dangerous, which denied
the worth of literature itself (or what we think of as creative writing).
    The psychological basis for the hostility can be found in Dryden's
friend Walter Charleton, who observed that in works of wit 'Phansie
ought to have the upper hand, because all Poems, of what sort soever,
please chiefly by Novelty.'⁷ How this remark becomes significant will
appear when it is set beside Charleton's definition of Fancy as the
faculty by which we conceive similarities 'in objects really unlike, and
pleasantly confound them in discourse: Which by its unexpected
Fineness and allusion, surprizing the Hearer, renders him less curious
or the truth of what is said.'⁸ In an age when the utilitarian and scien-
tific movement had grown to giant size, an art which pleased by con-
founding truth and deceiving men was bound to be viewed with
hostility. All wit came under attack.

³ Preface to *Annus Mirabilis*, in *Essays of Dryden*, ed. W. P. Ker, I, 14.
⁴ Antony Blackwall, *An Introduction to the Classics* (6th ed., 1746), p. 12.
⁵ *Ibid.*, p. 18.
⁶ *Discourse of Wit* (1685), p. 180.
⁷ *Brief Discourse concerning the Different Wits of Men* (1669), p. 25.
⁸ *Brief Discourse*, pp. 20–1.

The philosophic and moral basis for the hostility was well stated by Malebranche, who wrote: [9]

'But that which is most opposite to the efficacy of the Grace of Christ, is that which in the Language of the World is call'd Wit; for the better the Imagination is furnish'd, the more dangerous it is; subtilty, delicacy, vivacity and spaciousness of Imagination, great qualities in the Eyes of Men, are the most prolifick and the most general causes of the blindness of the Mind and the corruptation of the Heart. . . .'

In the few years preceding the publication of Pope's *Essay* the agitation concerning wit was intensified, partly because of the appearance of the *Letter concerning Enthusiasm* (1707) and *Sensus Communis* (1709), both of which, by pleading for the complete freedom of wit and raillery, even in the most serious matters, sent shivers of horror down the spines of some English and Continental readers. . . .

There soon issued a long and bitter retort called *Bart'lemy Fair: or, an Enquiry After Wit; In Which Due Respect Is Had to a Letter Concerning Enthusiasm* (1709). This work takes Shaftesbury's *Letter* to be primarily an assault on religion, and sees wit as a mode of enquiry that would unsettle everything, morals and government alike. Of the terrible menace lurking in wit the anonymous author bitterly remarks: 'To be Witty, if a Man knows how, is the only way to please. Wit is the Salt that gives a goût to any Carrion: Nothing so Profane, or Lewd, but shall be relish'd if it pass for Wit.'[10]

Such objections are obviously directed against, not true wit, but the abuse of it. Yet wit easily lent itself to abuse, and the contemporary mind distrusted it as a likely enemy to all goodness. With almost uncanny prescience the learned Dr Samuel Clarke answered part of Shaftesbury's contentions a few years before they were printed. In a series of sermons preached at St Paul's in 1705, he denounced the sort of men who pretend to seek for truth and to explode falsehood by means of wit.: [11]

'. . . whatsoever things are profane, impure, filthy, dishonourable and absurd; these things they make it their business to represent as harmless and indifferent, and to laugh Men out of their natural shame and abhorrence of them; nay, even to recommend them with their utmost Wit. Such Men as these, are not to be argued with, till they can be persuaded to use Arguments instead of Drollery. For Banter is not capable of being answered by Reason: not because it has any strength

---

[9] *A Treatise of Morality,* trans. James Shipton (1699), p. 114.
[10] P. 18.
[11] *Works of Samuel Clarke* (4 vols., 1738), II, 603–4.

in it; but because it runs out of all the bounds of Reason and good Sense, by extravagantly joining together such Images, as have not in themselves any manner of Similitude or Connexion; by which means all things are alike easy to be rendered ridiculous. . . .

Wit appeared to many good men as a threat to decency because it walked regularly with irreligion and vice. Thus James Buerdsell, fellow of Brasenose College, complained in 1700 that 'the prevailing Humour of Sceptism' had become 'so extreamly Modish, that no Person can be that self-admir'd thing, a Wit, without it.'[12] In the same year young Samuel Parker, of Trinity College, Oxford, deplored the sad fact that 'Dissoluteness and Irreligion are made the Livery of Wit, and no body must be conscious of good parts, but he loses the credit of them unless he take care to finish 'em with Immoralities.'[13] . . .

Much of the *Tatler* and *Spectator* papers was devoted to exposing false wit in social life, discrediting the antics of the unseemly biters and banterers, the scatterbrained and volatile, the uncouth leapers and slappers, the hollow laughers, the pert coxcombs. False wit in literature was attended to by Addison in the *Spectator*. Underlying these endeavours is the assumption that wit needed to be defended, and that it could be restored to its rightful place by stripping it of the gaudy and unclean adornments which thoughtless admirers had forced upon it. And at least since the time of Cowley's ode 'Of Wit,' the separation of true from false wit had been a regular mode of defending literature itself.

But besides these general reasons Pope had a personal stake in the argument over wit. The subject had interested him for years before the *Essay on Criticism* was published, as the correspondence with Walsh shows. It was in his correspondence with Wycherley, however, that the subject became crucial—and almost necessarily so. For in the late years of Dryden and the early years of Pope, Wycherley had become the very symbol of the poet of wit.

The trouble began with Wycherley's belated urge for recognition as a nondramatic poet, signalized by the publication in 1704 of his *Miscellany Poems*. Preceding the poems is a Preface that remains one of the unreadable wonders of our language. It is wit gone mad, an avalanche of simile and metaphor, a breathless flow of whim and fancy, out of which, now and then, there half emerges, here and there, a globule of meaning; after which a cloud of darkness settles, and the reader gropes his way blindly toward the poems that follow (where he is not to fare much better).

Little enthusiasm greeted the *Miscellany Poems*. But Wycherley,

[12] *Discourses and Essays on Several Subjects* (Oxford, 1700), p. 205.
[13] *Six Philosophical Essays* (1700), p. 18.

undaunted, commenced almost immediately to plan a new collection which should contain some unpublished verses and some revised and corrected versions of poems already printed. This time, however, he showed no unseemly haste in afflicting printer and public. Instead, he passed copies around to his friends for advice and correction. Among others so honoured was Alexander Pope.

Pope, as we know, took this responsibility seriously. In Wycherley's letter dated February 5, 1705–6[14] we discover that our bold youth was already pruning excrescences from the elder bard's disorganized fancies. On April 10, Pope was explaining with admirable candour that some of the poems were so wretched that 'to render them very good, would require a great addition, and almost the entire new writing of them.' Wycherley's chaos sprang from a false conception of wit. For great wits such as John Donne, said Pope, like great merchants take least pains to set out their valuable goods, where the 'haberdashers of small wit' spare no decorations to present their little wares as seductively as possible.[15] As the business of lopping and grafting proceeded, Wycherley's assumed meekness wore thin, until a minor explosion occurred in 1707. Pope had set about to produce a semblance of logical order in the poem on Dulness, subjecting it to radical alterations; such amiable helpfulness provoked Wycherley to this response on November 22:[16]

'And now for the pains you have taken to recommend my Dulness, by making it more methodical, I give you a thousand thanks, since true and natural Dulness is shown more by its pretence to form and method, as the sprightliness of wit by its despising both.'

Here was a home-thrust, impelled by some resentment and hostility. Pope's letter, dated one week later, shows that he was aware of the resentment; nevertheless he replied patiently: 'To methodize in your case, is full as necessary as to strike out; otherwise you had better destroy the whole frame, and reduce them into single thoughts in prose, like Rochefoucauld, as I have more than once hinted to you.'[17] As for the alleged incompatibility of wit and method, Pope urged that this is true only for the trivial forms of wit embodied in fancy or conceit; but as for true wit, which is propriety, why, that requires method not only to give perspicuity and harmony of parts, but also to insure that each detail will receive its increment of meaning and beauty from the surrounding elements.

This strange contest of wills lasted from 1706 until 1710 at least. In the latter year, on April 11, Wycherley wrote to Pope in protest against the extent to which the younger man was improving his verses. By

---

[14] Pope, *Works*, ed. Elwin-Courthope, VI, 26.
[15] Elwin-Courthope, VI, 28.
[16] *Ibid.*, VI, 33.
[17] *Ibid.*, VI, 34–5.

your tuning of my Welsh harp, he said, my rough sense is to become
less offensive to the fastidious ears of those finicky critics who deal
rather in sound than in meaning.[18] Wit shines with a native lustre that
defies the need of polish.

As Wycherley saw it, there was a generous, libertine spirit in wit,
too free to be confined, and too noble to be sacrificed for smoothness or
regularity. Taking form as a novel simile, a brilliant metaphor, a
dazzling paradox, or a smart aphorism, wit is its own justification
wherever it happens to appear. . . . To sacrifice . . . flashes of wit to an
ordered design, to a carefully conceived framework, is to sacrifice
poetry itself. . . .

Pope's artistic conscience told him that such scintillation, when it
failed to fit into its proper place and contribute to the effect of the
whole, was false wit because it was bad art. And he must have understood that such irresponsible, uncontrolled flashes, lacking any relationship with artistic purpose and solid sense, had contributed to the
disrepute into which wit had fallen. As he was driven to correct and
revise Wycherley's manuscripts, he was impelled to defend himself,
and true wit as well, by reaching a coherent view of literature that
would justify his own practice. It was a bold step for a virtually unknown young author to set himself against the most famous wit surviving from the glamorous court of Charles II. But he might draw
comfort and support from the fact that a few of the distinguished men
of the time had expressed concepts of wit similar to his own. Little by
little his ideas take form; we can see them developing in his correspondence, especially that with Wycherley. He told Spence later that
he had formulated the substance of the *Essay on Criticism* in prose
before he undertook the poem.

One passage in the poem that would seem to have Wycherley in
mind is that contained in lines 289–304, where he speaks of the
writers addicted to conceits and glittering thoughts, specious prodi-
galities which are valued by their creators not because they are essential parts of the meaning or because they fit into the places where they
are thrown, but because they startle and surprise or raise admiration
for their makers' liveliness. These are diseases. Works so constructed
are 'One glaring Chaos and wild heap of wit'—an extraordinarily apt
description of Wycherley's *Miscellany Poems* of 1704.

But there is a clearer and more specific connection between the
correspondence and the poem visible in the passage comprising lines
494–507. Here Pope describes the unhappiness that wit brings to
those who possess it by stirring up malice and envy in the dull and
ignorant. This, as we learn from a letter dated November 20, 1707,[19]

---

[18] *Ibid.*, VI, 44.
[19] *Ibid.*, VI, 32.

was a subject which he had treated in his reorganization of Wycherley's poem on Dullness. If his distinguished correspondent failed to appreciate the addition, nothing prevented the use of it in a new poem.

By an interesting association of ideas Pope proceeds from here, through a short transitional passage (lines 508-25) dealing with the shame and disgrace that wit suffers at the hands of its friends, to the conclusion of Part II. This concluding section (lines 526-55) completes the subject of Dullness and likewise fulfills the thought developed in lines 408-51, where Pope describes two types of false wit, one caused by servile dullness and the other by modes and current folly. In the closing lines of Part II two more kinds of false wit are exposed: that which grows out of the union of dullness with bawdry, and that which springs from dullness and irreligion. The interesting feature of Pope's strategy in this passage is that these two abuses of wit are made to appear as temporary phases in a historical process, the first brought about by the dissoluteness, luxury, and idleness in the reign of Charles II, and the second, by the license and impiety allowed in the reign of William III. These particular manifestations of false wit (both of them 'modes in wit' and 'current folly') are sharply dissociated from true wit by artfully fixing them in past reigns, which Pope had no need to defend, especially as, out of the Wit's Titans who flourished in these two reigns, the last surviving member and champion was none other than William Wycherley....

We must still ask ourselves, what did Pope mean by true wit, and what Augustan writers whose thoughts were taking a similar direction can help us to comprehend the import of his view?

In the course of exposing false wit, Pope suggests two criteria by which true wit may be determined. First, it belongs not to the part but to the whole. It is the master idea which informs every portion of the body and gives life and energy; it is the joint force of all components, and not the beauty, regularity, or brilliance of any one feature. It unites the parts, and prevents undue attention from falling on any one; and no part has goodness or badness in itself except in its relation to the whole. And if the whole is properly informed with wit, it gives a generous pleasure, warming the mind with rapture so that we are delighted though we know not why, so delighted that we cannot be disturbed by trivial faults in the execution.

The second test is, that it must take its course from nature, that is, from truth. But not necessarily from the worn or commonplace; enough that we recognize, when we encounter it in art, its essential agreement with the frame of our minds, with universal human experience. So far from being commonplace, the whole piece gives the effect of boldness, not because of style or artifice but because new life, energy, and insight have been added. It comes with the graces of expression, which tend to heighten the outlines of truth rather than to disguise or conceal them. The expression, in fact, should be as modestly plain as the subject and form permit; and sprightly wit is so far from adhering to it that the expression may rather be said to set off the wit. Nature alone is not true wit until it becomes animated and is drawn into a unity by the shaping spirit.

It is in Part I of the *Essay*, however, where we must look for a fuller account of the relationship of wit and art in the production of poetry.

Pope begins by specifying genius as the quality necessary in the poet, and taste in the critic, but notes that the two functions ideally should coincide. Genius is a synonym for wit, and after the first sixteen lines the former word is discarded in favour of the latter. Wit, then, is a quality that must be present at birth, and it is apportioned to men in varying measure and strength. If it is the genuine poetic gift, it may be fitted for only one type of poetry. Each man must discover his own special strength and cultivate only that for which he is specially fitted.

Along with genius (or taste) we can expect to find at least a rudimentary sense, or judgment, which is just as much the gift of heaven as wit. This sense needs developing; otherwise it is easily perverted, either by the formulas of academic learning or by the distortions of fashion. But nature, to protect us, herself provides the standard of good judgment: an impulse that leads us to prefer the lasting and universal over the ephemeral and local.

This thought is first suggested in lines 19–27, and is taken up again for further development in lines 68–87. Again we are assured that nature furnishes us with a just and universal standard of judgment. But nature also provides the life, force, and beauty that a work of genius requires; it is the source and end as well as the test of art. From this fund art draws its supplies, and proceeds quietly, unobtrusively, to endow all parts of the body with spirit and vigour.

At this point it is easy for the reader to become confused, for the principle of control, which at the start of the passage was called *judgment*, has now become *art*; a few lines later it appears as *wit*, and by the end of the passage it has been transformed back to *judgment* again. Perhaps the most perplexing lines are the oft-quoted:

> Some, to whom Heaven in wit has been profuse.
> Want as much more to turn it to its use. . . .

The lines lend themselves to ridicule, and Pope knew all too well that they left him open to banter. Yet, with his marvellous gift of lucidity to aid him, he left the couplet as we see it. Why? Presumably because it seemed to be the best way of putting something that was very difficult to express.

He found it difficult because it involved a question on which the credit of literature depended. For Pope's contemporaries, encouraged by Locke, were erecting a wall between wit and judgment and attempting to deposit the most valued achievements of mankind on the side of the wall occupied by judgment. This way of thinking is well described by Sir William Temple in his essay 'Of Poetry'. In the usual acceptation, he says, man's goal is taken to be profit or pleasure. The faculty of the mind conversant with profit is wisdom; that conversant with pleasure is wit (or the vein that produces poetry). To wisdom is attributed 'the Inventions or Productions of things generally esteemed the most necessary, useful, or profitable to Human Life'; and to wit, 'those Writings or Discourses which are the most Pleasing or Entertaining.[20] Wit may borrow from wisdom, of course, but its own proper role is to dazzle the eyes and tickle the ears and cut capers; it has no insight of its own, no peculiar way of thinking, nothing to offer but toys.

Into this pitfall Pope had no desire to plunge. Nor was he tempted by the compromise that seduced many of his contemporaries: to say that the essence of poetry is fable, design, or structure (product of the faculty to which we assign reason, judgment, and wisdom).[21] If the core of literature is provided by the plain rational faculty, then it is conceivable that whatever is valuable in it could be conveyed more profitably in another way (say, in plain didactic prose), without the fuss and feathers of literary art. But apart from that, the compromise effectively disinherits most of the kinds of poetry, for only epic, tragedy, and comedy necessarily have fables.

To Pope, wit and judgment, as they operate in literature, are married. In this union, so long as they are in a healthy state, they work together as a single faculty. As for the meaning of *wit* in the perplexed couplet, we must go back to the early lines in the poem, where we are told that genius and taste must ideally coincide; or, as the thought is expanded, that wit is accompanied by a rudimentary sense, potentially excellent, which requires development by experience. However great the gifts of heaven, wit, without that development, falls short of its perfection: natural wit needs training for its proper expression in art. But such training does not propose to foster an alien power, at odds with wit. Pope tries to make himself clear in the following passage (lines 88–140). The training designed to perfect the rudimentary sense is an experience of the great wit of the past, first through a study of the rules, in which the principles underlying the mighty achievements of the past art are set forth in simple abstraction; and second

[20] In Spingarn, III, 73–4.
[21] For a rather typical expression of the idea, see Mary Astell (?), *Bart'lemy Fair* (1709), p. 80: 'Colouring is the least of the Matter, both in Wit and Painting; a few bold Strokes never made an Artist; the Attitudes, Proportions, and above all the Design, shew the Masterly Genius.' Cf. also Dennis, *Critical Works*, II, 46.

by a detailed study of 'each Ancient's proper character' in every page of his work. Out of such experiences should come *literary* judgment, *literary* taste, which is the accomplished phase of wit; or, to put it in another way, wit in the writer is not merely the power to conceive of objects and endow them with 'Life, force, and beauty', but also the ability to find an appropriate style and form in which to express them; the latter ability, developed by knowledge of the rules and of master-pieces of literature, serves as taste and judgment. In the writer it is also art, invisibly guiding the energy of the conception so that it permeates the form and language, and achieves its desired end. Thus, if this sense (call it taste, judgment, or art) guides the creative energy and, in a way, contains it, nature is still the test of art, for this judgment must be constructed on the foundation of a natural artistic gift. And because this gift comes originally from Heaven, or nature, it may at times conduct the creative impulse to its objective by a route not recognized by the rules and untried by past masterpieces—so snatching a grace beyond the reach of art.

The important point is that Pope believed there was a special way of thinking peculiar to literature, a way called *wit*, which possessed unique values; he saw that wit (in the narrower sense) and judgment in the artist are but two aspects of a single way of thinking, and that judgment (or art) is not a churlish, rational censor but a natural literary sense cultivated by a wide acquaintance with literary masterpieces. Literature therefore is good, not because it charms eye or ear with sparkle and melody nor because it borrows wisdom from philosophy or science, but because wit, the unique mode of the literary artist, provides an insight into nature, endows it with 'Life, force, and beauty', and conveys it directly to our hearts, charming us as it makes us wiser.

The *Essay on Criticism*, then, had something to say. . . . But if we can follow what Pope says of wit, we can grasp his primary purpose. He had difficulty in expressing his ideas concerning wit because there existed no adequate critical vocabulary for him to draw upon. There did, however, exist a body of thought concerning wit, some expressions of which Pope was certainly acquainted with, and some part of which could serve to strengthen and clarify his own views. To the consideration of that body of thought it is reasonable that we proceed.

The first fact about wit that struck observers was that it made for a lively mind. Hobbes himself defined it as celerity of imagining, and thought of it as a tenuity and agility of spirits, which, as it distinguished its possessors from the dull and sluggish of soul, must to that extent have seemed to him as a virtue.[22] If wit meant nothing more than liveliness, it would have its value. Welsted, who liked to take an

----

[22] *Leviathan*, I, viii.

extreme position, remarked years later, partly out of admiration for sheer life and animation, that even the sprightly *nonsense* of wit is preferable to the dull sense of plodding, earth-bound creatures.[23]

A number of writers, however, refused to confine the liveliness of wit to sprightly nonsense. Liveliness, indeed, was the first quality that impressed the author of *Remarques on the Humours and Conversations of the Town* (1673), who described wit as 'properly the vivacity, and the agreeableness of the fancy'; nevertheless he adds immediately, 'yet there ought to belong something more to that high quality, than a little flash and quibble'.[24] 'Something more,' as he explains in the following pages, meant to him an intelligent subject, delivered 'sweet and pleasantly, in the native beauties of our Language'. In that high quality, true wit, we see, sense, liveliness, and worthy expression might coalesce. So likewise it appeared in the opinion of the great Robert Boyle, who remarked that wit, 'that nimble and acceptable Faculty of the Mind', involves both a readiness and subtlety in conceiving things, and a quickness and neatness in rendering them[25]—a way of putting the idea that neatly anticipates Pope's phrasing in a letter to Wycherley dated December 26, 1704: true wit is 'a perfect conception, with an easy delivery'.[26]

The vivacity of wit could be valuable for one of two reasons: either because it naturally operated to charm other minds, or because it was the mark of a soul capable of unusual powers, beyond the reach of ordinary men. There is a point at which vivacity and subtlety melt into swiftness and acuity. . . .

[Joseph Glanvill] castigates those who debase wit, which is truly fitted for 'great and noble Exercises of the Mind'. It is in reality, he remarks, 'a Faculty to dive into the depth of things, to find out their Causes and Relatives, Consonancies and Disagreements, and to make fit, useful, and unobvious Applications of their respective Relations and Dependencies.'[27] The simile and metaphor of literature, therefore, *may* become, not the trifling ornaments laid upon the truth, but instruments of the profoundest thinking, the natural way of revealing the discovery of hidden relationships. . . . Francis Atterbury, later a friend of Pope's, . . . discussed the subject in a sermon printed in 1708, while Pope was establishing his defences against Wycherley. Atterbury wrote, 'Wit, indeed, as it implies a certain uncommon Reach and Vivacity of Thought, is an Excellent Talent; very fit to be employ'd in the Search of Truth, and very capable of assisting us to discern

[23] *Epistles, Odes, &c* (1724), Dedication, p. xli.
[24] P. 93.
[25] *Occasional Reflections* (1665), p. 37.
[26] Elwin-Courthope, VI, 16.
[27] *A Whip for the Droll* (1700), pp. 4–5.

and embrace it. . . .'[28] His subsequent remarks show clearly that wit was not to be employed, as Shaftesbury proposed, in banter and raillery, to strip the mask from falsehood and thus arrive, indirectly, at truth; rather, it plunged straight to its object by virtue of its own range, acuity, and vivacity.

Even though Addison accepted Locke's definition of wit, thereby splitting off wit from judgment and demoting wit to the role of a mild spice serviceable in making morality pleasing to the palate, there were enough others who refused to be so misled. They persisted in thinking of wit as 'a high quality', fitted for 'great and noble Exercises of the Mind', as a special and valuable mode of apprehending nature and truth—not the plain and obvious, but the depth of things, where the complex relationships, the consonancies and disagreements, among the parts of nature lay open to wit alone. Some thought of judgment as a phase of wit; some thought of fancy as that part of wit which provided appropriate images and expression to deliver wit's discoveries. Wit and art are eternally wedded, and true wit is 'a perfection in our Faculties'.

This lofty conception of wit, making it possible to claim for literature a noble rank among human activities and a value far greater than can be granted that which merely entertains and pleases, was overshadowed in the early eighteenth century by the ideas of Locke and of men like him. And yet, sanctioned as it was by such formidable names as Robert Boyle, La Rochefoucauld, and Atterbury (some of whom were known to Pope), it offered an easily tenable position from which to defend literature from the assaults of those intent on debasing it. . . .

Certainly Pope intended to oppose any idea of wit that separated subject matter from style. It is significant that in a letter dated November 29, 1707, he defined wit, in 'the better notion of it', as propriety.[29] This, of course, was Dryden's definition, stated as early as 1677, and rephrased as 'thoughts and words elegantly adapted to the subject'.[30] It was Dryden's idea of wit to the end of his career, a definition which, as he says, 'I imagin'd I had first found out; but since am pleasingly convinc'd, that Aristotle has made the same Definition in other Terms.'[31] That Dryden's conception of wit interested other men than Pope at this time is strongly suggested by the *Tatler's* article from Will's Coffee-house which begins, 'This evening was spent at our table in discourse of propriety of words and thoughts, which is Mr Dryden's definition of wit . . .'[32]

[28] 'A Scorner Incapable of True Wisdom' (preached, 1694), in *Fourteen Sermons* (1708), pp. 158-9.
[29] Elwin-Courthope, VI, 34-5.
[30] *Essays of Dryden*, ed. W. P. Ker, I, 190; cf. also I, 270, and II, 9.
[31] 'Life of Lucian,' in *Works of Lucian* (1711), I, 42.
[32] *Tatler*, No. 62 (September 1, 1709).

The term *propriety* conveys no very clear idea to us when it is applied to literary criticism, and for that reason Dryden's definition has been taken much less seriously by modern scholars than it was by the Augustans. It deserves to be understood. The *Tatler* supposed, incorrectly, that it involved a relationship between thoughts and words only. In reality Dryden was urging a threefold relationship, between thoughts, words, *and* subject, effected in such a way that the three elements appear to belong to one another (*propriety* conveyed the sense of *ownership*); and the words 'elegantly adapted' point to the need of an active literary intelligence to produce the work of wit.

This account of wit as propriety bears a resemblance to an Augustan theory concerning the artistic process which may help to explain it. The theory, in brief, supposed that objects produce in genius (the artistic mind raised to a high degree of emotion and sensibility) certain thoughts which, in the very instant of their generation, take on forms and expression adequate to convey them and completely appropriate to them. A form of the theory can be found in the works of Dryden's young friend, John Dennis. In the genius, says Dennis, 'as Thoughts produce the Spirit, the Spirit produces and makes the Expression; which is known by Experience to all who are Poets . . .'[33] The expression (which includes style, harmony, rhythm, etc.), then, is not the result of a separate act but exists in the most intimate and necessary relationship with the ideas, emotions, and attitudes of the artist, being engendered along with them. The thoughts do not become wit until they are animated and transfused by the shaping spirit which gives them expression—and all elements take form in perfect propriety.

To define wit, therefore, as 'What oft was thought, but ne'er so well expressed', does not say or imply that wit is a stale or commonplace thought nicely tricked out. The definition rather supposes that the writer, starting with a common and universal experience, sees it in a new light; and his sensitive spirit, endowing it with life and fresh meaning, provides it with form, image, language, and harmony appropriate to it. It presupposes the liveliness and insight of the creative mind; and it demands propriety, the perfect agreement of words, thoughts (as reshaped by the artist), and subject. The result is nature, and it is wit.[34]

---

[33] *Advancement and Reformation of Modern Poetry* (1701), in *Critical Works*, I (Baltimore, 1939), 222.

[34] The tendency to define wit in terms of the thoughts produced, or to emphasize the necessary presence in wit of common sense, is well illustrated by Bouhours, who in *Les Entretiens d'Ariste et d'Eugene* (Paris, 1737), p. 258, defined wit as: '*C'est un corps solide qui brille. . . .*' It is no accident that Bouhours, after a neglect of three decades, was becoming influential in England by 1710. Garth had recommended him to Oldmixon, as he probably had to Pope; and Addison in the *Spectator* was to proclaim him the greatest of the French critics. Although Bouhours in *La Maniere de Bien Penser* seemed to lay

When Pope composed the *Essay on Criticism*, there was need for a defence of wit—and that is to say, of literature as well. His own circumstances, involved as he was in a controversy with the most famous writer surviving from the court of Charles II and what was understood to have been the golden age of wit, demanded that he should justify his bold and rash treatment of Wycherley. Locke's conception of wit was of no use to him; in fact, it served the enemy better. But there were other ideas available which were consistent with a conviction of the high dignity and noble function of literature. Through this maze Pope attempted to thread his way. If he was not entirely successful in conveying his meaning with utter clarity, the fault lay partly in the lack of a critical vocabulary. But he had something important to say, and there are good clues to his intention. Pope saw, thought, felt, and wrote as the complete artist. Those who would like to understand his views of the literary art (and of criticism, its complement) must read the *Essay on Criticism* with a fuller awareness of its historical setting.

From 'Pope on Wit: The *Essay on Criticism*,' in *The Seventeenth Century: Studies in the History of English Thought and Literature from Bacon to Pope*, by R. F. Jones and others writing in his honour, Stanford, 1951, pp. 225–46.

heavy stress on common sense and the logical element in wit, he made it clear that he was really concerned not with thought but with the turn given the thought by the ingenious mind and with the appropriateness of the style and language to that turn or attitude. Common sense did not strike him as wit until it was vivified and illuminated by the author. This much Pope and Bouhours had in common; in what remains, Pope's superior artistic sense is obvious.

IAN JACK

The Rape of the Lock

... UNLIKE *MacFlecknoe*, *The Rape of the Lock* contains very few of the directly 'diminishing' images of straightforward satire.[1] Far more numerous are mock-heroic images which enhance the effect of the fundamental irony.

> Not fierce *Othello* in so loud a Strain ...
> Roar'd for the Handkerchief that caus'd his Pain.[2]

as Belinda called for the ravished lock.

> [As] Ladies in Romance assist their Knight,
> Present the Spear, and arm him for the Fight,[3]

so Clarissa hands the fatal scissors to Lord Petre. The apotheosis of the lock is illustrated from Roman myth:

> So *Rome's* great Founder to the Heav'ns withdrew,
> To *Proculus* alone confess'd in view.[4]

The game of ombre is dignified by several elaborate similes (notably that which compares the scattering of the cards to the dispersal of a 'routed Army'),[5] as is the battle of the *beaux* and *belles*:

> So when bold *Homer* makes the Gods engage,
> And heav'nly Breasts with human Passions rage;
> 'Gainst *Pallas*, *Mars*; *Latona*, *Hermes* Arms;
> And all *Olympus* rings with loud Alarms.
> *Jove's* Thunder roars, Heav'n trembles all around;
> Blue *Neptune* storms, the bellowing Deeps resound:
> *Earth* shakes her nodding Tow'rs, the Ground gives way;
> And the pale Ghosts start at the Flash of Day.[6]

'A game of romps was never so well dignified before.'[7]

---

[1] Examples, however, may be found at i. 100 and iv. 54.
[2] v. 105–6.   [3] iii. 129–30.   [4] v. 125–6.
[5] iii. 81–6.   [6] v. 45–52.   [7] Warton, i. 248.

Such are the images which one expects to find in a mock-heroic poem. Less simple in its effect is the comparison of Belinda to the sun at the beginning Canto II:

> Not with more Glories, in th'Etherial Plain,
> The Sun first rises o'er the purpled Main,
> Than issuing forth, the Rival of his Beams
> Launch'd on the Bosom of the Silver *Thames*.

There is a paradox about this image which is the paradox about the whole poem. In the simple mock-heroic, of which *MacFlecknoe* is a good example, the subject of the poem is compared to something great and made ridiculous by the comparison. It is 'a sort of [deliberate] transgression against the rules of proportion and mechanicks: it is using a vast force to lift a *feather*'.[8] The comparison of Shadwell to Hannibal is, simply, comic; and the result is denigration. The comparison of Belinda to the sun is different. It is a wild exaggeration, hardly less absurd for being a commonplace image in love poetry; and Pope was fully aware of its absurdity. But it is not merely absurd: it contains an element of the same imaginative truth as the line

> *Belinda* smil'd, and all the World was gay.[9]

What is true of the comparison of Belinda to the sun is true of the whole conception of *The Rape of the Lock*. There is an element of the incongruous in comparing a pretty girl to the sun and describing her life in the style appropriate to the adventures of a hero, but it is a different incongruity from that created by comparing Shadwell to Hannibal and describing his 'coronation' in the heroic style. While the heroic idiom of *MacFlecknoe* merely ridicules, the heroic idiom of *The Rape of the Lock* has its measure of appropriateness as well as of inappropriateness. Eighteenth-century theorists referred to the 'dignity' with which the mock-heroic treatment of a trivial subject invests it: whereas in *MacFlecknoe* this dignity is wholly ironical, in *The Rape of the Lock* it is not. . . .

The moral of *The Rape of the Lock* must not be forgotten. If he meant to include the poem amongst the early work in which 'pure Description held the Place of Sense',[10] Pope was being deliberately unfair. *The Rape of the Lock* is itself the best evidence that 'Sense' may be expressed by means of a 'fable' and made more vivid by narrative and description. For all his delight in the beauty of Belinda's world Pope never allows it to arrogate the place which rightly belongs to the sovereignty of Sense.

The full complexity of his attitude may be examined in the lines

[8] I have adapted a sentence from para. xxi of the Postscript to the *Odyssey*.
[9] ii. 52.
[10] *Epistle to Dr. Arbuthnot*, I. 148.

in which 'Belinda dressing is painted in as pompous a manner, as Achilles arming':[11]

> And now, unveil'd, the *Toilet* stands display'd,
> Each Silver Vase in mystic Order laid.
> First, rob'd in White, the Nymph intent adores
> With Head uncover'd, the *Cosmetic* Pow'rs.
> A heav'nly Image in the Glass appears,
> To that she bends, to that her Eyes she rears;
> Th'inferior Priestess, at her Altar's side,
> Trembling, begins the sacred Rites of Pride.
> Unnumber'd Treasures ope at once, and here
> The various Off'rings of the World appear;
> From each she nicely culls with curious Toil,
> And decks the Goddess with the glitt'ring Spoil.
> This Casket *India*'s glowing Gems unlocks,
> And all *Arabia* breathes from yonder Box.
> The Tortoise here and Elephant unite,
> Transform'd to *Combs*, the speckled and the white.[12]

Pope delights in the 'artificial beauty' that he is describing. Yet he passes a judgment, which is expressed by the imagery of the whole passage. Just as Ben Jonson makes Volpone condemn himself out of his own mouth by apostrophizing Gold in idolatrous terms, so in the description of the toilet-table Pope shows Belinda lavishing on her own beauty the adoration which should be reserved for a higher object. Pope acknowledges the beauty of the scene, and paints it brilliantly; yet he reminds the reader that the rites he is describing are those 'of *Pride*'.[13] In the thought of the eighteenth century pride remained the first of sins. By making it 'sacred' Belinda, and the whole *beau monde* which she represents, is guilty of a serious moral fault. Pope's moral judgment is implicit throughout. . . .

If it had lacked a moral, explicit or implicit, *The Rape of the Lock* would have failed to meet one of the basic demands of Augustan heroic theory. . . . In a deep sense the moral of a poem is its significance, the expression on the countenenace of the events which it describes. Its insistence on a moral was not the least of the ways in which the theory of the mock-epic helped Pope to develop his occasional poem on a lovers' tiff until it became what Warton justly called 'the BEST SATIRE extant'.[14]

From *Augustan Satire: Intention and Idiom in English Poetry 1660–1750*, Oxford, 1952, chap. V, pp. 77–96.

[11] Warton, i. 230.   [12] i. 121–36.
[13] The word 'Pride' occurs eight times in the course of the poem, several of these being in key passages. 'Proud' and 'the Proud' also occur, as do 'Vain' and 'Vanities'.
[14] i. 254.

AUSTIN WARREN

The Rape of the Lock as Burlesque

... THE most successful reconciliation of classicism and rationalism, or poetry and philosophy, or the incorrect, great past and the neater, thinner present, took place in terms of burlesque. Burlesque is often mask, often humility. The mock-epic is not mockery of the epic but elegantly affectionate homage, offered by a writer who finds it irrelevant to his age. As its signal advantage, burlesque (with its allied forms, satire and irony) allows a self-conscious writer to attend to objects, causes, and persons in which he is deeply interested yet of which, in part or with some part of him, he disapproves. 'Interest' is a category which subsumes love and hate, approval and disapproval; very often it is an unequal, an unsteady mixture. Burlesque covers a multitude of adjustments; and each specimen requires to be separately scrutinized and defined. ...

The neoclassical theory of serious diction called for a thinly honorific vocabulary, for adjectives which singled out an obvious attribute implicit in the noun—the 'verdant' meadow, the 'blue' violet—or were devised as loosely decorative epithets—the 'pleasing' shades, the 'grateful' clusters, the 'fair' fields: all examples from the *Pastorals*. The inhibitions, imposed upon the joint authority of Philosophy and the Ancients, are stringent. Words must not be ambiguous or multiple-meaninged (for then they become puns, and puns are forms of verbal wit, and verbal wit is 'false wit'); they must not be homely or technical (since poetry addresses men *as such*—gentlemen, not specialists in science or labourers); they must be lucid (for poetry owes its kinship with philosophy to its universality).

These inhibitions are removed or greatly mitigated, however, when the poet does not profess poetry but only an epistle or a burlesque imitation. The difference is notable in the *Moral Essays*, the *Rape*, the *Dunciad*.

> But hark! the chiming clocks to dinner call;
> A hundred footsteps *scrape* the Marble Hall;

> The rich buffet well-coloured serpents grace,
> And *gaping* Tritons *spew* to wash your face.
>
>   .   .   .
>
> Whether the nymph shall break Diana's law,
> Or some frail China jar receive a flaw;
> Or stain her honour, or her new brocade;
> Forget her prayers, or miss a masquerade;
> Or lose her heart, or necklace, at a ball.

Zeugma, the joining of two unlike objects governed by a single verb, is of course a form of pun; yet this verbal play constitutes one of Pope's most poetic resources in the *Rape*: it is this device, one might say, which gives the tone to the whole.

Burlesque are both Pope's masterpieces, the *Rape* and the *Dunciad*. Of the mock-epic, we may provisionally say that it plays form against matter, a lofty and elaborate form against a trivial situation or set of persons or theme. But 'form against matter' is too simple a naming. The real failure of the post-Miltonic epic lay, surely, in the supposition that the heroic poem could be written in an unheroic age; that a poem which, generally, involved the interrelation of the human and the divine, the natural and the supernatural, could be written in an age when 'thinking people' had grown too prudent for heroism, too sophisticated for religion. John Dennis, whose taste among the Ancients was for Homer, Pindar, and Sophocles, and among the Moderns for Milton, was not unsound in his critical contention that great poetry like that of his favourites must be religious. So we might restate the incongruity as between heroic things and refined, between an age of faith and an age of reason. The mock-epic reminds an unheroic age of its own nature: by historical reference, it defines the 'civilized' present.

Is Pope, then, satirizing Belinda's world? Yes, but lightly. His intent is rather to juxtapose contrasting modes than to decide how far his aristocracy has gained by its elegance, how far lost by its safe distance from war, politics, poverty, and sin. The poem is in nothing more dexterous than in its controlled juxtaposition of worlds. In another context we should find ominous those brilliant lines which couple by incongruity the worlds of the bourgeoisie and the proletariat with that of the leisure class:

> The hungry Judges soon the sentence sign,
> And wretches hang that jury-men may dine;
> The merchant from th' Exchange returns in peace,
> And the long labours of the Toilet cease.

The *Rape* owes its richness and resonance to its overstructure of powerful, dangerous motifs. What keeps it from being that filigree

F

artifice which the romantics saw (and praised) is its playing with fire, especially the fires of sex and religion. Though Pope was scarcely a 'good Catholic', his parents were devout; and he is writing of an 'old Catholic' society; and many of his effects involve the suggestion of blasphemous parallels: the linking of English folklore and the Lives of the Saints, and of both to his gentle mythology of urbane 'machines'. He links the nurse's moonlit elves and fairy ring with the priest's tales of 'virgins visited by Angel-powers'; the visions of the Cave of Spleen are

> Dreadful as hermit's dreams in haunted shades,
> Or bright as visions of expiring maids,

visions which may or may not be reducible to physiological disturbances; the Baron and Belinda have their altars to Pride and Love, their real religions.

What, for religion, is got by parody parallel is, for sexual morality, managed by insinuation. Though it is admitted that nymphs may break Diana's law, we see none do so; the titular *Rape* is but of a lock. The opening of Canto III (a preview for the *School for Scandal*) shows the chorus at work ('At every word a reputation dies'); but we do not hear the death. A characteristic passage of *double-entendre* retails the difficulty of preserving a 'melting maid's' purity at such a time and place of temptation as the midnight masquerade, while assuring us that her male companions' Honour, or her sylph, preserves her virtue.

Without doubt the specific perspectives through parody and irony are purposed. But there may be doubt whether these effects are not local and episodic, unsubject to central design and all-governing tone; for, though silly things have been said about Pope's work of composition (as if 'closed couplets' must all be equally discrete and unreconciled), he was, of course, so intent on making every verse exciting and finished as to make it difficult for the poem to subordinate them. In the case of the *Rape* he is often in danger but, I think, unvanquished. What organizes the poem is not exclusively the narrative, with its chronological and dramatic sequence of scenes (including two battles); it is yet more its tone—the steadiness with which it holds, against heroic and religious perspectives, to its seriocomic view of a little elegant society.

Not to the manor born, Pope makes the drawing-room seem an achievement. He so treats a woman's day, says Johnson, that 'though nothing is disguised, everything is striking; and we feel all the appetite of curiosity for that from which we have a thousand times turned fastidiously away.' Pope had not turned fastidiously away; like Proust, another 'outsider', he was fascinated by the ritual which gave—or signified—the aristocratic status. He has practised, on other matter, the Wordsworthian formula of giving to the unmarvellous the light of wonder. Society is a wonder, we are made to feel; convention a triumph of happy contrivance; coffee a luxury; a card game a crisis. This effect is in large measure the result of the 'machinery' of sylphs, who not only contrast with Homer's and Milton's 'machines' but parallel Pope's women—those coquettes, termagants, dociles, and prudes whose natures they abstract and stylize.

The burlesque of the *Rape* provides, then, an elaborate stratification of attitudes and effects: amusement and trifles taken seriously; delight at elegance; recollections of earlier literature (Homer and Spenser) in counterpoint against the current literary mode; juxtaposition of corresponding worlds (Achilles' shield, the great petticoat); reminders of the economic and political structures which make possible this leisure-class comedy, of the moral and religious structures which make possible a society at all. . . .

From Chapter 3 of *Rage for Order*, Chicago, 1948, pp. 37–51.

MAYNARD MACK

The Muse of
Satire

... IN this essay, ... my thesis will be that even in these apparently
very personal poems, [the formal satires such as *Arbuthnot*] we overlook what is most essential if we overlook the distinction between
the historical Alexander Pope and the dramatic Alexander Pope who
speaks them.

It is to underscore this distinction that I have ventured in my title
to name the Muse. For the Muse ought always to be our reminder
that it is not the author as man who casts these shadows on our printed
page, but the author as poet: an instrument possessed by and pos-
sessing—Plato would have said a god, we must at any rate say an art.
And, moreover, the Muse ought to remind us that in any given instance
the shadow may not delineate even the whole poet, but perhaps only
that angle of his sensibility which best refracts the light from epic,
elegy, pastoral, lyric, satire. The fact is not without significance, it
seems to me, that though Pope, following the great victories of
naturalism in the seventeenth century, had to make do with a mini-
mum of mythology and myth, he never discarded the Muse, either
the conception or the term. She appears with remarkable regularity
even in his satires, and there, for my present purposes, I am choosing
to regard her as a not entirely playful symbol of the impersonality of
the satiric genre—of its rhetorical and dramatic character.

Rhetorically considered, satire belongs to the category of *laus et
vituperatio,* praise and blame. It aims, like all poetry, in Sidney's
phrase, through the 'fayning notable images of vertues [and] vices',
to achieve 'that delightful teaching which must be the right describing
note to know a Poet by'. And it has, of course, its own distinctive means
to this. Prominent among them to a casual eye is the *exemplum* in the
form of portrait, like Dryden's Zimri or Pope's Atticus; and the middle
style, which stresses conversational speech (more than passion or
grandiloquence) along with aphoristic phrasings, witty turns, and
ironical indirections. Less prominent but more important than either
of these is the satiric fiction into which such materials must be built.

All good satire, I believe it is fair to say, exhibits an appreciable degree of fictionality. Where the fiction inheres in familiar elements like plot, as in *Absalom and Achitophel* or *The Rape of the Lock* or *The Dunciad* or *The Beggar's Opera*, its presence is, of course, unmistakable; and it is unmistakable, too, in such satires as Swift's *Argument against Abolishing Christianity* or his *Modest Proposal*, where the relation of the speaker to the author is extremely oblique, not to say antithetical. But when the relation is only slightly oblique, as in Pope's formal satires, the fictionality takes subtler forms and resides in places where, under the influence of romantic theories of poetry as the spontaneous overflow of powerful emotions, we have become unaccustomed to attend to it. . . .

One aspect of the fictionality in Pope's case resides in the general plan of the formal satiric poem. This . . . contains always two layers. There is a thesis layer attacking vice and folly, elaborated with every kind of rhetorical device, and, much briefer, an antithesis layer illustrating or implying a philosophy of rational control, usually embodied in some more or less ideal norm like the Stoic *vir bonus*, the good plain man. The contours of a formal verse satire, in other words, are not established entirely or even principally by a poet's rancorous sensibility; they are part of a fiction.

We encounter a further aspect of this fiction when we pause to consider that the bipartite structure just mentioned apparently exists to reflect a more general fictive situation. This situation is the warfare of good and evil—differentiated in satire from the forms it might take in, say, lyric, by being viewed from the angle of social solidarity rather than private introspection; and from the forms it might take in, say, tragedy, by being carried on in a context that asserts the primacy of moral decision, as tragedy asserts the primacy of moral understanding.

Tragedy and satire, I suspect, are two ends of a literary spectrum. Tragedy tends to exhibit the inadequacy of norms, to dissolve systematized values, to precipitate a meaning containing—but not necessarily contained by—recognizable ethical codes. Satire, on the contrary, asserts the validity and necessity of norms, systematic values, and meanings that *are* contained by recognizable codes. Where tragedy fortifies the sense of irrationality and complexity in experience because it presents us a world in which man is more victim than agent, in which our commodities prove to be our defects (and vice versa), and in which blindness and madness are likely to be symbols of insight, satire tends to fortify our feeling that life makes more immediate moral sense. In the world it offers us, madness and blindness are usually the emblems of vice and folly, evil and good are clearly distinguishable, criminals and fools are invariably responsible (therefore censurable), and standards of judgment are indubitable. All this, too, results from a slant of the glass, a fictional perspective on the real world—which, as we know, does not wholly correspond either with the tragic outlook or the satiric one.

Finally, we must note, among these general and pervasive aspects of fictionality in satire, the *ethos* of the satirist. Classical rhetoric, it is well to recall, divides the persuasive elements in any communication from one man to another into three sorts: the force of the arguments employed, the appeal to the interest and emotions of the hearer, and the weight of authority that comes from the hearer's estimate of the speaker's character, his *ethos*. For the satirist especially, the establishment of an authoritative *ethos* is imperative. If he is to be effective in 'that delightful teaching,' he must be accepted by his audience as a fundamentally virtuous and tolerant man, who challenges the doings of other men not whenever he happens to feel vindictive, but whenever they deserve it. On this account, the satirist's *apologia* for his satire is one of the stock subjects of both the classical writers and Pope: the audience must be assured that its censor is a man of good will, who has been, as it were, *forced* into action. *Difficile est saturam non scribere*: 'It is difficult *not* to write satire'.

Moreover, the satirist's *ethos* is the *rhetorical* occasion (even though vanity may be among the *motives*) of his frequent citations of himself. As a candid fellow, for instance, and no pretender to be holier than thou:

> I love to pour out all myself, as plain
> As downright Shippen, or as old Montaigne....
> In me what Spots, (for Spots I have) appear,
> Will prove at least the Medium must be clear.

A man, too, of simple tastes, persistent loyalties:

> Content with little, I can piddle here
> On Broccoli and mutton, round the Year;
> But ancient friends, (tho' poor, or out of play)
> That touch my Bell, I cannot turn away.

A man whose character was formed in the good old-fashioned way by home instruction and edifying books:

> Bred up at home, full early I begun
> To read in Greek, the Wrath of Peleus' Son.
> Besides, My Father taught me from a Lad,
> The better Art, to know the good from bad.

Consequently, a man who honours the natural pieties:

> Me, let the tender Office long engage
> To rock the Cradle of reposing Age:

who is sensible of life's true ends:

> Farewell then Verse, and Love, and ev'ry Toy,
> The rhymes and rattles of the Man or Boy,
> What right, what true, what fit, we justly call,
> Let this be all my Care—for this is All:

and who is valued by distinguished friends. If the friends happen to be out of power, or drawn in part from a vanished Golden Age, so much the better for *ethos*: our satirist is guaranteed to be no time-server.

> But does the Court a worthy Man remove?
> That instant, I declare, he has my love.
> I shun his Zenith, court his mild Decline;
> Thus Sommers once, and Halifax were mine.
> Oft in the clear, still Mirrour of Retreat
> I study'd Shrewsbury, the wise and great. . . .
> How pleasing Atterbury's softer hour!
> How shin'd the Soul, unconquer'd in the Tow'r!
> How can I Pult'ney, Chesterfield forget
> While Roman Spirit charms, and Attic Wit? . . .
> Names which I long have lov'd, nor lov'd in vain,
> Rank'd with their Friends, not number'd with their Train.

By passages of this kind in Pope's satires, the rhetorically innocent are habitually distressed. They remark with surprise that Pope insists on portraying himself in these poems as 'lofty, good-humoured, calm, disinterested'. Or they grow indignant that an epistle like *Arbuthnot* reveals 'not what Pope really was, but what he wished others to think him'. They fail to notice that he speaks this way only in a certain kind of poem, and so enlarge irrelevantly—though to be sure with biographical truth enough—upon the subject of his vanity. Meantime, on a rhetorical view, the real point remains, which is simply that in passages of this sort, as also in his notes to the *Dunciad*, and probably, to some extent, in the publication of his letters (both these enterprises, significantly, accompanied his turning satirist), Pope felt the necessity of supporting the *ethos* a satirical poet must have. . . .

This *persona* or speaker has almost always in Pope's formal satires three distinguishable voices. One is the voice of the man I have partly described in connection with *ethos*: the man of plain living, high thinking, lasting friendships; who hates lies, slanders, lampoons; who laughs at flatteries of himself; who is 'soft by Nature, more a Dupe than Wit'; who loves of all things best 'the Language of the Heart'; and who views his own poetry with amused affection qualified with Virgilian tenderness for the tears of things in general:

> Years foll'wing Years, steal something ev'ry day,
> At last they steal us from ourselves away;
> In one our Frolicks, one Amusements end,
> In one a Mistress drops, in one a Friend:
> This subtle Thief of Life, this paltry Time,
> What will it leave me, if it snatch my Rhime?

Then, secondly, there is the voice of the *naïf*, the *ingénu*, the simple heart: 'the Prejudice of Youth'. The owner of this voice is usually the vehicle of ironies about matters he professes not to understand, and is amazed by his own involvement in the literary arts. 'I lisp'd in Numbers, for the Numbers came'—says this voice, speaking of one of the most carefully meditated poetries in literature. Or else: 'Why did I write? What sin to me unknown Dipt me in Ink...?' To the owner of this voice, his proficiency in satire is particularly puzzling. Should it be explained as the by-product of insomnia?

> I nod in Company, I wake at Night,
> Fools rush into my Head, and so I write;

a scheme of personal defence like jujitsu?

> Satire's my weapon...
> Its proper pow'r to hurt each Creature feels,
> Bulls aim their Horns, and Asses lift their Heels;

or is it a species of harmless madness, a kind of psychosomatic twitch that nothing short of death will stop?

> Whether the darken'd Room to Muse invite,
> Or whiten'd Wall provoke the Skew'r to write,
> In Durance, Exile, Bedlam, or the Mint,
> Like Lee and Budgell, I will Rhyme and Print.

Pope's third voice is that of the public defender. If the first voice gives us the satirist as *vir bonus*, the plain good private citizen, and the second, the satirist as *ingénu*, this one brings us the satirist as hero. A peculiar tightening in the verse takes place whenever this *persona* begins to speak, whether he speaks of the mysterious purpose of

> That God of Nature, who, within us still,
> Inclines our Action, not constrains our Will;

or of the time when

> Inexorable Death shall level all,
> And Trees, and Stones, and Farms, and Farmer fall;

or of his own calling:

Yes, I am proud; I must be proud to see
Men not afraid of God, afraid of me.

The satirist as *vir bonus* was content to laugh at flatteries, but the
satirist as hero feels differently:

Fr. This filthy Simile, this beastly Line,
Quite turns my Stomach—P. So does Flatt'ry mine;
And all your Courtly Civet Cats can vent,
Perfume to you, to me is Excrement.

Similarly, the satirist as *ingénu* chose to find the motives of satire
in a nervous reflex; the satirist as hero has other views:

O sacred Weapon! left for Truth's defence,
Sole dread of Folly, Vice, and Insolence!
To all but Heav'n-directed hands deny'd,
The Muse may give thee, but the Gods must guide.

Without pretending that these are the only voices Pope uses, or
that they are always perfectly distinguishable, we may observe that
the total dramatic development of any one of his formal satires is
to a large extent determined by the way they succeed one another,
modulate and qualify one another, and occasionally fuse with one
another. In a poem like Pope's imitation of the first satire of Horace's
second book, the structure is in a very real sense no more than a function of the modulations in tone that it takes to get from the opening
verses, where the *naïf* shows up with his little slingshot and his five
smooth pebbles from the brook:

Tim'rous by Nature, of the Rich in awe,
I come to Council learned in the Law;

through the point, about a hundred lines later, at which we realize
that this fellow has somehow got Goliath's head in his hand (and also,
the hero's accents in his voice):

Hear this, and tremble! you, who 'scape the Laws.
Yes, while I live, no rich or noble knave
Shall walk the World, in credit, to his grave;

then back down past a window opening on the unimpeachable integrity
of the *vir bonus*, instanced in his ties with men whom it is no longer
fashionable to know: 'Chiefs, out of War, and Statesmen, out of
Place'; and so, finally, to a ressumption of the voice of the *ingénu*,
surprised and pained that he should be thought to have any but the
noblest aims. 'Libels and Satires!' he exclaims, on learning the category into which his poems are thrust—'lawless things indeed!'

> But grave Epistles, bringing Vice to light,
> Such as a King might read, a Bishop write,
> Such as Sir Robert would approve——?

Indeed? says the friend; well, to be sure, *that's* different: 'you may then proceed'.

Though the construction in Pope's satires is by no means always so schematic as in this example, it seems almost invariably to invoke the three voices of the *naïf*, the *vir bonus*, and the hero. And their presence need not perhaps surprise us, if we pause to consider that they sum up, between them, most of what is essential in the satirist's position. As *naïf*, the satirist educates us. He makes us see the ulcer where we were accustomed to see the rouge. He is the child in the fairy story forever crying, 'But mamma, the king *is* naked'. As *vir bonus*, on the other hand, he wins our confidence in his personal moral insight. He shows us that he is stable, independent, urbane, wise—a man who knows there is a time to laugh, a time to weep: 'Who would not weep, if Atticus were he?' And finally, as hero, he opens to us a world where the discernment of evil is always accompanied, as it is not always in the real world, by the courage to strike at it. He invites us, in an excellent phrase of Mr Bredvold's, to join 'the invisible church of good men' everywhere, 'few though they may be—for whom things matter'. And he never lets us forget that we *are* at war; there *is* an enemy.

We should never have made, I think, so many mistakes about a portrait like 'Sporus' if we had grasped the fact that it is primarily a portrait of the enemy (one of the finest Pope ever drew), evoked in a particular context at a particular point. We know, of course, that the lines were based on Pope's contemporary, Lord Hervey, whom he passionately disliked; and therefore we may justly infer that personal animus entered powerfully into their motivation.

But to read with this animus as our centre of interest is to overlook the fact that, though the lines may be historically about Hervey, they are rhetorically about the enemy. It is to fail to see that they sum up in an *exemplum* (of which the implications become very pointed in the references to Satan) the fundamental attributes of the invader in every garden: his specious attractiveness—as a butterfly, a painted child, a dimpling stream; his nastiness—as a bug, a creature generated in dirt, a thing that stinks and stings, a toad spitting froth and venom; his essential impotence—as a mumbling spaniel, a shallow stream, a puppet, a hermaphrodite; and yet his perpetual menace as the tempter, powerless himself but always lurking 'at the ear of Eve', as Pope puts it, to usurp the powers of good and pervert them. Because the lines associate Sporus with Evil in this larger sense, his portrait can be the ladder by which Pope mounts, in the evolution of the epistle as a whole, from the studiedly personal impatience of the pestered private citizen in the opening lines: ' "Shut, shut the door, good John!" fatigu'd I said', to the impersonal trumpet tones of the public defender on the walls of *Civitas Dei*—'Welcome for thee, fair Virtue, all the past'. Without Sporus prostrate on the field behind him, the satiric speaker could never have supported this heroic tone. Something pretty close to the intensity exhibited by this portrait was called for, at just this point, not by the poet's actual feelings about a contemporary, but by the drama of feelings that has been building inside the poem—the fictive war—'the strong Antipathy of Good to Bad', here projected in its climactic symbol.

From 'The Muse of Satire', in *The Yale Review*, vol. XLI, no. 1, 1951, pp. 80–92.

ELIAS F. MENGEL

Patterns of Imagery in Pope's *Arbuthnot*

IN his ' "Wit and Poetry and Pope": Some Observations on his Imagery' Maynard Mack speaks of Pope's wide variety of patterns 'that help supply the kind of unity which he is popularly not supposed to have.'[1] *An Epistle to Dr Arbuthnot* offers striking illustration of this conception: analysis reveals patterns of images running throughout, each one discrete yet all so related as to give to the whole a metaphoric value which helps to tie the poem together. I do not mean to suggest that *Arbuthnot* has no other kind of unity apart from that given to it by these patterns of imagery, or that this imagery functions autonomously.[2]

Five main images emerge, all connected in a kind of evolution: animal-filth-disease-persecution-virtuous man. The animal image yields the filth, the noxious element out of which disease arises, disease turns into persecution, and persecution reveals the virtuous man.

The animal image comprises all references to animals, worms, and insects in the poem, that is, to any sentient being below man. The basis of this image seems to lie in the association of the poetasters with 'low Grubstreet'. To Pope these men write and act without thinking, in automatic response to certain stimuli: they are like trained hawks, 'May Dunce by Dunce be whistled off my hands!' (254),[3] or like frogs that live on flies, wordcatchers that live on syllables (166). Furthermore, like spiders (89), they live in their own filth, so that disease flourishes in Grubstreet. From there in swarms and packs the creatures descend on Pope, carrying their infection with them. Pestered as he is by these flatterers and foes, he cannot keep from slapping in self-defence. Thus Pope justifies satire from a man of

---

[1] In *Pope and His Contemporaries, Essays Presented to George Sherburn*, ed. James L. Clifford and Louis A. Landa (Oxford, 1949), p. 33.

[2] For an analysis of the rhetorical (oratorical) unity of *Arbuthnot* the reader is referred to Elder Olson, 'Rhetoric and the Appreciation of Pope,' *MP*, xxxvii (1939–40), 13–35.

[3] The *OED* cites Burton's *Anatomy of Melancholy* II.ii.iii.317, 'As a long-winged Hawke when he is first whistled off the fist, mounts aloft.'

peace. It is not spiteful or inhumane to slap a mosquito or beat off a mad dog. He suffers fools with the greatest patience and restraint, but, stung beyond endurance, he is forced to cry out. And when he finally does lash out, there is something heroic in his flapping fools and whipping scoundrels regardless of their rank. However, he is far from bellicose: he keeps apart from the warfare of the wits. It is by stressing this proud aloofness ('I kept, like *Asian* Monarchs, from their sight,' 220) that Pope can make the transition to his final picture of himself as *vir bonus*, full of love, nursing his aged mother and asking Heaven's blessing for his friend. This is the culminating image of this *apologia* for his life and art in that it represents the furthest remove from the popular conception of the satirist as a malevolent man.

The drama of the poem begins with a wry and casual tone, leads up gradually to a high pitch of indignation in the Sporus portrait, and closes on the even higher plane of serenity, all passion spent. Within this rhetorical sequence Pope's patterns of imagery work in such a way as to direct the movement. By skilfully playing off one against the other the comic and serious sides of these images, by making minor fluctuations between the comic and the serious, Pope controls the tone of his poem and brings about a gradual movement from gay to grave. . . .

The Portrait of Sporus

The disgust which has been gradually built up from the opening lines by the interrelated patterns of animals and filth . . . finally bursts forth, untempered by comic admixture, in the scorn of the Sporus portrait:

> Let *Sporus* tremble—'What? that Thing of silk,
> '*Sporus,* that mere white Curd of Ass's milk?
> 'Satire or Sense alas! can *Sporus* feel?
> 'Who breaks a Butterfly upon a Wheel?'
> Yet let me flap this Bug with gilded wings,
> This painted Child of Dirt that stinks and stings;
> Whose Buzz the Witty and the Fair annoys,
> Yet Wit ne'er tastes, and Beauty ne'er enjoys,
> So well-bred Spaniels civilly delight
> In mumbling of the Game they dare not bite.
> Eternal Smiles his Emptiness betray,
> As shallow streams run dimpling all the way.
> Whether in florid Impotence he speaks,
> And, as the Prompter breathes, the Puppet squeaks;
> Or at the Ear of *Eve,* familiar Toad,
> Half Froth, half Venom, spits himself abroad,

> In Puns, or Politicks, or Tales, or Lyes,
> Or Spite, or Smut, or Rymes, or Blasphemies.
> His Wit all see-saw between *that* and *this*,
> Now high, now low, now Master up, now Miss,
> And he himself one vile Antithesis.
> Amphibious Thing! that acting either Part,
> The trifling Head, or the corrupted Heart!
> Fop at the Toilet, Flatt'rer at the Board,
> Now trips a Lady, and now struts a Lord.
> *Eve's* Tempter thus the Rabbins have exprest,
> A Cherub's face, a Reptile all the rest;
> Beauty that shocks you, Parts that none will trust,
> Wit that can creep, and Pride that licks the dust.
>
> (305–33)

In this greatest concentration of animal images in the poem one notes a climactic progression, an accumulation of disgust. In the beginning Sporus is beneath contempt as almost non-existent, but by the end of the portrait he is a filthy, abhorrent creature. To Arbuthnot he is simply a thing of silk, a mere white curd of ass's milk, a butterfly. But to Pope he is a gilded bug that stinks and stings, or a fawning spaniel, a hunter taught to cringe from killing. Then, all beauty and delicacy gone, he becomes an ugly, filth-spitting toad, an importunate, malicious toady like Satan 'close at the eare of *Eve*', and finally a snake, Satan on his belly in the dirt. In this gradual building up of loathing, the Sporus portrait recapitulates the movement of the animal-filth connection of which it is both the end and the climax.[4]

Upon reaching this pitch of feeling Pope drops for good his mask of irony and shows himself the solemn and righteous man. Now he can speak of himself in the third person and in an exalted mode:

> Not Fortune's Worshipper, nor Fashion's Fool,
> Not Lucre's Madman, nor Ambition's Tool,
> Not proud, nor servile, be one Poet's praise
> That, if he pleas'd, he pleas'd by manly ways. (334–7)
> 'But why insult the Poor, affront the Great?'
> A Knave's a Knave, to me, in ev'ry State,
> Alike my scorn, if he succeed or fail,
> *Sporus* at Court, or *Japhet* in a Jayl. (360–3)

The remainder of the poem gradually refines away the scorn that emanates from the Sporus passage by stressing Pope's patience and piety. The keynote of this last movement is sounded in the following couplet:

[4] Cf. l. 170, 'Of hairs, or straws, or dirt, or grubs, or worms.' Here, too, the local progression points to the general movement.

> Yet soft by Nature, more a Dupe than Wit,
> *Sapho* can tell you how this Man was bit. (368–9)

Far from being mean and spiteful, this dreaded satirist is even gullible. Furthermore, he suffers meekly for Virtue's sake the foulest slanders:

> Full ten years slander'd, did he once reply?
> Three thousand Suns went down on *Welsted*'s Lye. (374–5)
> Let the *Two Curls* of Town and Court, abuse
> His Father, Mother, Body, Soul, and Muse. (380–1)

In the wistful description of his father's life which follows, Pope not only demonstrates a proper filial devotion, but also announces his own ideal life, the life of peace on a few paternal acres:

> Stranger to Civil and Religious Rage,
> The good Man walk'd innoxious thro' his Age....
> By Nature honest, by Experience wise,
> Healthy by Temp'rance and by Exercise:
> His Life, tho' long, to sickness past unknown,
> His Death was instant, and without a groan.
>
> (394–5, 400–3)

Here in the implied contrast between his father's Arcadian life and that which he himself is doomed to lead we have the climax of the disease and persecution images. The father, in the noiseless tenor of his way, knew nothing of the plagues from which the son is suffering. His was a life of wholesome simplicity and peace, whereas Pope's existence is full of anguished groans. Sick himself, he is made worse by his sick civilization.

Finally, the love and yearning of this passage is brought to an even higher pitch in the prayer-like close, the climax of the good man image and thus of the poem itself. Here with the heightened style the interjection 'O' is natural, the low 'death-bed' is raised to the 'Bed of Death', and the last word is 'Heav'n':

> O Friend! may each Domestick Bliss be thine!
> Be no unpleasing Melancholy mine:
> Me, let the tender Office long engage
> To rock the Cradle of reposing Age,
> With lenient Arts extend a Mother's breath,
> Make Langour smile, and smooth the Bed of Death, ...
> Whether that Blessing be deny'd, or giv'n,
> Thus far was right, the rest belongs to Heav'n.
>
> (406–11, 418–19)

From 'Patterns of Imagery in Pope's *Arbuthnot*', in *P.M.L.A.*, vol. LXIX, no. 1, 1954, pp. 189–97.

R. A. BROWER

The
Moral Essays

THE doubts that occur in reading even the best parts of the *Essay on Man* disappear completely when we turn to one of the great passages in the *Moral Essays*:

> At Timon's Villa let us pass a day,
> Where all cry out, 'What sums are thrown away'
> So proud, so grand, of that stupendous air,
> Soft and Agreeable come never there.
> Greatness, with Timon, dwells in such a draught
> As brings all Brobdignag before your thought.
> To compass this, his building is a Town,
> His pond an Ocean, his parterre a Down:
> Who but must laugh, the Master when he sees,
> A puny insect, shiv'ring at a breeze!
>   (*Epistle to Burlington*, 99–108)

Here is the *élan* and rapture of genius, of a poet moving freely and yet with perfect control, compressing into a few lines a great variety of rhythmic and dramatic effect with swift changes of irony and brilliant contrasts of image. The passage goes easily from the grand narrative swing of the first couplet to the resounding oratorical architecture of preposterous praise, to the small-voiced thrust of the last murderous line. The irony of exaggerated compliment, 'So proud, so grand ...' gives way first to the muted politeness of 'Soft and Agreeable come never there', then rises to a tremendous Swiftian parody of Milton,

> As brings all Brobdignag before your thought.

The final reduction of 'Greatness' is cinematographic, the eye shifting from Vanbrughian monstrosity to the mean and almost charmingly microscopic. We are left with an impression not of vindictiveness, but of fantastic agility creating a vision of the grossness and littleness of man's attempt to raise himself by conspicuous consumption.

The *Epistle to Burlington*, from which these lines come, shows much more certainly than the *Essay on Man* that Pope had now found his true subject and form as a mature poet. He is not the poet of systematic reason and reasoning, but of man and of the free play of intelligence over the human scene. The *Epistles to Several Persons*, as they were originally called, are much more important as poetry than the more ambitious poem that proclaims 'Man' as its subject, since in these more casual pieces Pope attained a variety and wholeness of expression equalled only in the two extremes of his art, the *Rape of the Lock* and the Fourth Book of the *Dunciad*. All four essays are rich compositions in irony, and two, *To Burlington* and *To a Lady*, are masterpieces. While there are signs in the other two of the strain between 'philosophy' and sensibility that mars the *Essay on Man*, both poems show Pope trying to express a complex if precarious vision of man and society. . . .

The essential poetic design[1] of the *Essays* can be seen most clearly in the first in order of writing, the epistle addressed to Burlington, the amateur architect and publicist for Palladian architecture and the new more 'natural' manner of gardening in which Pope had a special interest. The poem moves along conversationally through exempla of bad taste to reflections and hints on good taste, to the grand narrative-portrait of Timon and the brief epilogue in which Burlington is hailed as the author of 'Imperial Works, and worthy Kings'. In its broad outline and type the poem is Horatian, as can be seen from the briefly sketched portraits in the first half of the poem, the casual introduction of pieces of doctrine, and the concentration in the second half on a single bad case and its nobler opposite. But the poetic life and the more subtly Horatian quality of the epistle come out in the masterly variation of tones, with all the attendant ironies.

Speaking as one aristocratic amateur to another, Pope allows himself the lordly freedom of conversational intimacy ('you'd' and 'you'll') and also some upper-class vulgarity ('spew' and 'squirt'). But the voice heard throughout the conversation, which holds the poem together, is one of polite Roman cultivation. It is the tone inherent in the dramatic situation of the poem and in the cultural situation of Augustan England: Pope speaks as Horace to Burlington as Maecenas. (Burlington, we might note, gave Pope some stone for his villa and a good deal of advice, if not the villa itself.) The Roman character of the voice is brought out through casual reference to the paraphernalia of ancient culture—'hecatombs', 'quincunxes', and 'Tritons', through pompous exclamations and commands associated with Roman satirical and prophetic styles, and finally by parody of various classical styles,

---

[1] The following description of the design is a considerably revised and shortened version of my analysis in *The Fields of Light*, New York, 1951, pp. 138–63.

G

heroic, pastoral-descriptive, and elegiac. Similar tones, most of them touched with the Roman accent, keep recurring and with them go recurrent ironies. Two or three examples will give some sense of the rich variety of devices and ironic effects. Here, for instance, is a satiric comment on Timon's manners, which is created by simultaneous parody of Pope and Milton:

> My Lord advances with majestic mien,
> Smit with the mighty pleasure, to be seen ... (127-8)

Compare *Paradise Lost*,

> Smit with the love of sacred Song ...

and Pope's *Iliad*,

> And smit with Love of Honourable Deeds.

The sound of 'smit'—ugly because of the morpheme and its associations—makes the literary echo sound like a vulgar wisecrack, an effect underlined by the crude bathos of 'to be seen'. In a later passage, a neat allusion to Greek myth is wittily compressed into a single word of exotic flavour, a device similar to Dryden's use of resounding Greek and Latin cognates:

> In plenty starving, *tantaliz'd* in state ... (163)

The scene of Timon's dinner opens with an heroic announcement and continues in language associated with ancient architecture and religious ceremonies, diction at once under-cut by hints of modern grossness:

> But hark! the chiming Clocks to dinner call;
> A hundred footsteps scrape the marble Hall:
> The rich Buffet well-colour'd Serpents grace,
> And gaping Tritons spew to wash your face. (151-4)

A subtler irony is then created by high-flying rhetorical questions matched with seemingly more august 'classical' answers:

> Is this a dinner? this a Genial room?
> No, 'tis a Temple, and a Hecatomb.
> A solemn Sacrifice, perform'd in state,
> You drink by measure, and to minutes eat. (155-8)

The play of antithetical wit is particularly apt in a poem satirizing the clash between ideal and actual in the antics of these latter-day Romans. The attitude of ironic wonder, conveyed here through question and answer, is kept up through the poem by all sorts of devices and quiet pressures, from Pope's usual 'marvelling' exclamations to exaggerated praise and fine understatement, but underneath the irony

there is always a more or less direct allusion to the Roman achievement and an ideal civilization.

The irony in the dinner scene and in many other passages is descriptive as well as allusive, and Pope gives fine pictorial impressions
of the buildings and gardens whose owners he is satirizing, as in these
lines reminiscent of *Windsor Forest*:

> Behold Villario's ten-years toil compleat;
> His Quincunx darkens, his Espaliers meet,
> The Wood supports the Plain, the parts unite,
> And strength of Shade contends with strength of Light;
> A waving Glow his bloomy beds display,
> Blushing in bright diversities of day ... (79–84)

There is also a hint of self-parody in the last line, which is lifted
without change from Pope's imitation of Cowley, perhaps his earliest
garden-piece. The sensuous quality of what is seen is active even when
the language is ambiguously 'aesthetic'. The billowy splendours of
baroque painting survive the mockery of

> On painted Ceilings you devoutly stare,
> Where sprawl the Saints of Verrio or Laguerre,
> On gilded clouds in fair expansion lie,
> And bring all Paradise before your eye ... (145–8)

where the painters' unconscious parody of a great style (quite appropriate in this travesty of religion) is suggested through the happy ambiguity of 'sprawl' and 'expansion' and through parody of Milton.

> And bring all Heav'n before mine eyes.
> *(Il Penseroso,* 166)

Timon's garden is a caricature of Pope's early descriptive manner,
'a designed scene' with a vengeance, but in spite of the mechanical
absurdities, the picture has the romantic charm of one of those
eighteenth-century landscapes where classical sculptures lie in a tangle
of vines and flowers:

> Here Amphitrite sails thro' myrtle bowers;
> There Gladiators fight, or die, in flow'rs;
> Un-water'd see the drooping sea-horse mourn,
> And swallows roost in Nilus' dusty Urn. (123–6)

By similar uses of pictorial imagery at many points in the poem Pope
creates a vague continuity of metaphor: we feel that the visual beauties of nature are 'picturesque' in the simplest sense of the term, and
beyond the particular images we feel quite distinctly the larger metaphor of Nature as 'Great Designer' or 'Designing Power'. Through
this permeating analogy, and especially through recurrent patterns of

tone and irony, Pope builds up a unity of style expressive of unity of
vision.

The importance of rhythmic patterns recurring along with the same
or similar patterns of image and irony can be easily seen by comparing
different parts of the epistle. When ironic meanings become violently
antithetical, Pope uses the same patterns of exact balance that accen-
tuate the symmetries of art in more descriptive passages. In the account
of the clock-like service at Timon's dinner, there is the same obnoxious
symmetry of words and stresses as in the earlier picture of his gardens.
The inversion of time is expressed by the rhetorical figure used to
depict the inversion of nature:

> You drink by measure, and to minutes eat. (158)

> Trees cut to Statues, Statues thick as trees . . . (120)

With the return of the familiar ironic contrast we hear a swing and a
pause, a grouping of accents and syllables already associated with that
particular type of irony. In addition to such *reprises* of irony-
with-metrical pattern, there is the larger compositional rhythm of separate verse paragraphs, which is especially clear in purely ironic con-
texts. The shorter portraits and the individual paragraphs of the
Timon narrative tend to develop in much the same way. Ordinarily
Pope opens at the top of his tonal scale, often with an exclamation or
some semi-heroic note, and descends at the end to a semi-vulgar conversational level. Toward the middle of the verse-paragraph comes
a pictorial phase with balanced beauties that so easily become balanced incongruities, but in the last couplet or two the ironic pretence
of beauty and consistency is given up, and nobility and politeness of
tone completely disappear:

> The thriving plants ignoble broomsticks made,
> Now sweep those Alleys they were born to shade. (97–8)

Some such development, with many fine variations in detail, may be
traced in nearly all of the more satirical passages of the poem. . . .

The continuities I have been describing—far too schematically—
would be of little more than formal value if they were not the living
medium through which Pope expresses a larger vision of art and
society and an important criticism of builders and cultivators of the
arts. As in all serious irony the force of local ironies depends on a
vibrant reference to what James calls 'the ideal other case', in the
Epistle to Burlington, to the cultural ideal implied in the dramatic
texture of the poem, as in Pope's address to Burlington:

> You show us, Rome was glorious, not profuse,
> And pompous buildings once were things of Use. (23–4)

Here is the poem's imaginative germ, the nucleus of its felt relationships. The ideal that ratifies the ironies and makes them meaningful
is the type of aesthetic and social behaviour implicit in addressing
Burlington as an aristocrat and restorer of Roman and Renaissance
principles of architecture, implicit too in the Latinate accent of
'profuse' and 'pompous', in the balancing of values, and in the corresponding formality of verbal pattern. As further expressed in the closing section of the poem, the ideal is that of the responsible aristocrat
who builds and plants for socially useful ends, whose whole style,
in acting as a public benefactor and in designing and building, is
Roman. Unlike 'Imitating Fools' he considers the propriety of classical design to its modern use. His 'pompous buildings' owe their
'Splendour' to his 'Sense':

> 'Tis Use alone that sanctifies Expence,
> And Splendour borrows all her rays from Sense. (179–80)

'Good Sense', the faculty indispensable for classical propriety, is
equally necessary for the exercise of a larger propriety, for 'following
Nature':

> Good Sense, which only is the gift of Heav'n,
> And tho' no science, fairly worth the seven:
> A Light, which in yourself you must perceive;
> Jones and Le Nôtre have it not to give.
>
> To build, to plant, whatever you intend,
> To rear the Column, or the Arch to bend,
> To swell the Terras, or to sink the Grot;
> In all, let Nature never be forgot.
> But treat the Goddess like a modest fair,
> Nor over-dress, nor leave her wholly bare;
> Let not each beauty ev'ry where be spy'd,
> Where half the skill is decently to hide.
> He gains all points, who pleasingly confounds,
> Surprizes, varies, and conceals the Bounds.
>
> Consult the Genius of the Place in all;
> That tells the Waters or to rise, or fall,
> Or helps th' ambitious Hill the heav'ns to scale,
> Or scoops in circling theatres the Vale,
> Calls in the Country, catches opening glades,
> Joins willing woods, and varies shades from shades,
> Now breaks, or now directs, th' intending Lines;
> Paints as you plant, and, as you work, designs (43–64)

The relevant meanings of 'Sense' and 'following Nature' can be
gathered as in the *Essay on Criticism* from metaphor and imagery as
much as from the direct statements. It is worth noting that 'Sense'

is an inner 'Light', and 'the gift of Heav'n', not acquired by learning, but an inborn power, essentially aristocratic. The true gardener is a poet of the landscape who in Horace's words, *omne tulit punctum* not by excessive ornament, but by bringing out the 'living grace' of things, both their beauty and their 'pleasing confusion'. It is also significant that 'the Genius of the Place' is described in imagery borrowed from painting and drawing. To 'follow Nature' in gardening as in Wit is to work with the artistry of Nature the Designer. Vaguely enough for us, but in terms clear to readers of the *Essay on Man*, Pope is again alluding to nature as the principle of order in all things, an order that includes spontaneous variety. If the architect-gardener works according to Nature's order,

> Parts answ'ring parts shall slide into a whole,
> Spontaneous beauties all around advance . . . (66–7)

This generous concept of propriety in design that imitates the grand artistry of nature and that includes 'surprise' is inseparable from the remembered image of ancient art and the Roman-aristocratic code with its stress on appropriateness of design to use. (We might note that for Horace the beautiful garden is a useful one.)

The connexion between Pope's modes of expression and the cultural ideal is not a relation between ideas, or between ideas and devices, but a connexion continually being renewed in the resonances of words, a peculiarly poetic experience of language. The finest examples of this active relationship come in the noble epitaph that closes the satire on Timon's monstrosities:

> Another age shall see the golden Ear
> Imbrown the Slope, and nod on the Parterre,
> Deep Harvests bury all his pride has plann'd,
> And laughing Ceres re-assume the land. (173–6)

The impersonality and formality of tone with its Latinate 'laughing Ceres' and 're-assume the land' belong to the voice of the idealized aristocrat: it is not Pope himself who speaks. The pictorial imagery brings to mind the 'design' of Nature and the noble builder's aim of imitating its varied order in his creations. The future scene will be one of useful art, of fields that are picturesque in cultivation, not stupidly landscaped nor abandoned to 'wild disorder'. 'Gold', symbolic in Timon's villa of waste and impropriety, is in this setting a symbol of 'Splendour' that 'borrows all her rays from Sense'. 'Laughing Ceres' signifies among other things the Nature of cultivated fields smiling in mocking triumph over waste and the 'inversion' of nature. In using a phrase that echoes the *laeta seges* of the *Georgics*, Pope reminds us that his vision of nature and art and society has a great historical model. . . .

Horace and the Moral Epistles

We cannot of course rule out direct moral statement from poetry, least of all from the poetry of Pope; but there are ways and ways of stating in poetry, and much depends on what happens elsewhere in the poem in which statements occur, on the kind of commerce set up as in Shakespeare between 'truth' and drama, including the quiet drama of the Horatian epistle. In the *Epistle to Burlington,* the commerce is active and unforced, since the voice of the aesthetic and social philosopher is recognizably the same as that of the amused observer of Timon and his kind. The *Epistle to Bathurst* offers important social and moral criticism made through symbolic portraits of such power as to undercut the avowed philosophy of the epistle. In the *Epistle to Cobham,* Pope's most serious concern, the inscrutability of human nature, is expressed in lively exempla or in finely ironic poses and symbolic imagery. As in Horace the beliefs that lie deepest in the epistle are continually being enacted in the fine 'gestures' of style. But the official doctrine of the ruling passions has only a slight connexion with Pope's dominant attitudes and modes of expression in the poem. In the *Epistle to a Lady* Pope approaches the view of human nature implicit in the *Epistle to Cobham,* but he has now fully recovered his integrity of vision and expression: he will write no more *Essays on Man.*

It seems inevitable and right to invoke the image of Horace in connexion with the poem that in total effect comes nearer to an Horatian epistle than anything Pope has yet written. In writing of the characters of women Pope is philosophic in Horace's most characteristic manner, and the burden of the poem is thoroughly Horatian—an expression of mingled amusement and horror at the muddle most people make of their lives and of rare satisfaction in finding one life, like Horace's Ofellus or Volteius, that seems to make sense. It is Horatian too in Pope's refusal to be dazzled by social prestige or pretension to wisdom, and in his quiet testimony to deep but free and easy friendship. The epistle is also Horatian in its poetic art, in the placing of contrasting cases that culminate in a winning yet not over-serious portrait of an ideal, in establishing a tone of casual talk that can embrace literary parody and high allusion, and finally in the skilful handling of transitions, which for Pope as for Horace is not only a technique of style, but a technique of moving freely among moral and emotional possibilities.

From *Alexander Pope: The Poetry of Allusion,* Oxford, 1959, Chap. 8, pp. 240–81.

THOMAS R. EDWARDS

Light and Nature: A Reading of *The Dunciad*

ALTHOUGH the simple joke at the heart of the *Dunciad* is the same joke Pope uses in the *Rape of the Lock*—if you describe small, bad people with the language you ordinarily use to describe the largest and best people the human mind can conceive of, the result will be disastrous to the former—still it is obvious that in the *Dunciad* the effect of the joke has changed.[1] Take, for example, this passage, with its startling reversal of the normal process of purity yielding to decay:

> Thro' Lud's fam'd gates, along the well-known Fleet,
> Rolls the black troop, and over-shades the street,
> 'Till show'rs of Sermons, Characters, Essays,
> In circling fleeces whiten all the ways:
> So clouds replenish'd from some bog below,
> Mount in dark volumes, and descend in snow (II, 359–64).

The simile demands a complex response, combining revulsion at the Dunces' corruption ('bog'), wonder at their stupid but stubborn perseverance (it must be hard to make even fake snow from such dirty material), pleasure in the poetic power that can bring a kind of beauty out of such ugliness, and amusement that the comparison is used at all. This last feeling differs, however, from the amusement evoked by epic parody in the *Rape of the Lock*; while the *Dunciad* has a beauty of its own, it is far from the almost child-like pleasure in small, glittering things expressed by the earlier poem. Pope's use of incongruity is becoming less simply comic—laughter at clouds being replenished from bogs will be just a little nervous.

Uncomfortable juxtapositions of the conventionally pleasant and the ugly run through the poem. The remarkably profuse imagery comparing men to animals elaborately relates the world of the Dunces to the lower orders of creation; and although in part we feel superior to the Dunces because we are human, reasonable, and so forth, we have

[1] This article deals with the 1743 version of the poem in four books; all quotations are taken from *The Dunciad*, ed. James Sutherland, 2nd ed., London and New Haven, 1953.

at the same time to concede them a certain mindless but disturbingly potent vitality. Pope has other ways of suggesting that to be a Dunce is to have given up all meaningful ties with ordinary nature, thus ceasing to be human. The world of Dulness is full of monstrous distortion—in Book I (81–4), for example, the goddess proudly views her 'wild creation' of 'momentary monsters', who are elsewhere compared to statues and machines. If they retain a semblance of humanity, some deformity or other will mark them as Dulness's own, as in the case of the 'meagre, muse-rid mope, adjust and thin' (II, 37), Defoe earless in the pillory (II, 147), or the Virtuoso who is 'canker'd' as his Coins' (IV, 349); if they still look fully human, they are much embarrassed (IV, 525–8). Perhaps the richest vein of distortion runs in the allusions to monstrous births and perverse familial relations, for Dulness is the 'Mighty Mother', and her maternity implies a dreadful change in the normal processes of fruition and growth:

> Here she beholds the Chaos dark and deep,
> Where nameless Somethings in their causes sleep,
> 'Till genial Jacob, or a warm Third day,
> Call forth each mass, a Poem, or a Play:
> How hints, like spawn, scarce quick in embryo lie,
> How new-born nonsense first is taught to cry (I. 55–60).[2]

The reference is to *literary* deformity, to be sure, but the imagery invites a response that seems too strong for the reference—Pope asks us to react to bad writing as powerfully as we react to departures from natural birth and growth.

The most famous and most often deplored kind of ugliness in the *Dunciad* is of course the obscenity, the way in which Pope dwells upon the excretory processes and debased sexuality. The delicate sexual innuendoes of the *Rape of the Lock* give way to vigorous expressions of interest in the obscene and all its details:

> Renew'd by ordure's sympathetic force,
> As oil'd with magic juices for the course,
> Vig'rous he rises; from th' effluvia strong
> Imbibes new life, and scours and stinks along;
> Re-passes Lintot, vindicates the race,
> Nor heeds the brown dishonours of his face (II, 103–8).

The elegant irony of 'sympathetic', the mouth-filling Latinate diction (e.g., 'vindicate' in the sense of 'lay claim to'), and the neat epic parody

---

[2] For other instances of this kind of distortion, see I, 69–70, 121–6, 311–16; III, 313–4.

H

in 'brown dishonours'[3] combine in a deceptive sonority of movement
that makes the bite of 'scours and stinks' and 'brown' especially im-
polite. Pope's artistry struggles with our revulsion and subdues it,
and the result is richly poetic, but 'comedy' is not precisely the word
for what happens. Though we must probably laugh at Curll in order
to avoid some more painful response, the vision of a human being
drawing sustenance from filth cannot simply seem amusing. The
struggle between tonal dignity and conceptual ugliness produces a
degree of imaginative violence that would have torn the *Rape of the
Lock* to pieces; in this new poetic context violent personal feeling
seems to be making decorous public discourse almost impossible.

The rhetorical situation that lies behind such uses of ugliness
seems an elaborate one. Everyone knows that Pope was a relentless
hater, and there has always been a strong suspicion (to put it mildly)
that the *Dunciad* represents only its author's personal animosity towards most of the Augustan literary world. Yet the poem seems much
more impressive than a product of mere spite should. Its violence
may in fact be seen as dramatic rhetoric of a rich and powerful sort—
Pope is 'guaranteeing' the moral validity of his hatred by refusing to
disguise or gloss it over in any decorous way. It is as though he were
saying: 'Half measure won't do; the honest man eventually finds that
stupidity and vanity are intolerable, and he must speak out strongly
against them even if social decorum be violated.' The voice that speaks
in the Dunciad is that of the compulsive truth-teller; when we know
that it is *Pope* who has adopted this role, that the master of the barbed
needle has had to take up the pole-axe, matters seem desperate.

The style of the *Dunciad* cannot of course be accounted for by so
crude a label as 'ugliness'. On the one hand, we are to take the deformed, depraved world of Grub-street as an image of the actual
world we ourselves inhabit, or of what it may become if Dulness pre-
vails. At the same time, however, Pope keeps reminding us that Grub-
street may be a special and limited world surrounded by saner, more
pleasant realms of order. The surface of negative ugliness is balanced
by various modes of positive assertion that work beneath it.

This doubleness, as has often been remarked, appears in the texture
of the verse:

> So, (fam'd like thee for turbulence and horns,)
> Eridanus his humble fountain scorns,
> Thro' half the heav'ns he pours th' exalted urn;
> His rapid waters in their passage burn (II, 181–4).

The beautiful elevation and movement of the last line modulates the

---

[3] Compare 'the long-contended Honours of her Head' (*Rape of the Lock*
IV, 140) and the discussion of the formula by Geoffrey Tillotson, *On the
Poetry of Pope*, 2nd ed., Oxford, 1950, pp. 154–5.

disgust we may feel for the action and for the further obscene suggestion in 'burn' (which Scriblerus carefully underlines in a note). It
is as though Pope could not help writing beautifully, whatever the
occasion. As Dr Leavis says, the beauty of such a passage 'is inseparable from the whole habit of versification.... When Pope is
preoccupied with the metrical structure, the weight, and the pattern
of his couplets, he is bringing to bear on his "materials" habits of
thought and feeling, and habits of ordering thought and feeling. The
habits are those of a great and ardent representative of Augustan civilization.'[4] This is surely true; and we might add that Pope's habits
serve a rhetorical purpose of which he must have been aware. The
ability to find beauty in ugliness, without obscuring the fact that it *is*
ugly, is expressive of the highest form of civilized intelligence, and it
triumphantly asserts Pope's superiority, in sensibility and moral
soundness, to his victims. Dunces make ugliness from beauty, and the
difference between their activity and the contrary activity dramatized
in the verse itself marks the distinction between anarchy and order.

This undercurrent of positive values takes a number of forms. Pope
plays off Grub-street ugliness against the heroic dignity of classical
epic, the artfully beautiful innocence of pastoral, the rich fertility of
actual nature, and the moral seriousness of the classical and Christian
traditions in general. Such contrasts both underline the squalor of the
Dunces' world and enhance the gravity of their offence, which is in
effect an attempt to subvert human and natural order.

Darkness and Light

The contrast between the ugliness of Dulness and the beautiful
dignity of human reason seems to be the primary theme of the *Dunciad*.
It can be seen, I have suggested, as a stylistic principle operating in
isolated passages—as, for example, when an obscene image is balanced
by 'classical' tone or rhythm. It operates, however, in larger ways as
well, and indeed lends to the complete four-book version of 1743 a
kind of unity that has not been fully appreciated, as a study of a central
symbolic contrast may help to show.

The prominence of *darkness* in the *Dunciad* has been pointed out,
most satisfactorily perhaps by G. Wilson Knight, but the extent to
which the opposition between darkness and light pervades and directs
the poem has not received the attention it should have.[5] The key passage is of course the famous conclusion, in which Pope suddenly aban-
dons the elaborate fictions of mock epic to turn his eyes upon the

[4] F. R. Leavis, *The Common Pursuit*, London, 1952, p. 90.
[5] See G. Wilson Knight, *Laureate of Peace*, London, 1954, pp. 57–8.
Rebecca Price Parkin, *The Poetic Workmanship of Alexander Pope*, Minneapolis, 1955, pp. 116–23, considers the light imagery from a different point of
view than mine.

cosmos. At line 627 of Book IV (Pope provides a row of asterisks to mark the division) the Dunces vanish entirely as the poet turns his attention from the puny creatures of Dulness to the larger and more general implications of the intellectual and moral disorder he has been criticizing. Parody and vituperation yield to an intensely felt depiction of the death of reason and humanistic value, expressed in a way that recalls the Christian treatment of Doomsday. The reader is no longer an unimplicated observer and evaluator, as Pope adopts direct address and the present tense in an effort to involve us personally in his sudden revelation of what nonsense ultimately leads to. A certain dramatic neatness is lost by transferring this prophetic speech from Settle, who spoke it as the conclusion of the earlier three-book versions, to the anonymous narrator, but there is a compensating gain in dramatic seriousness. When Settle says it we tend not to believe him—it seems the product of a Dunce's deranged imagination; but when it is spoken by the narrator himself, and so backed by all the resources of feeling that have informed the poem, we must consider it at face value.[6]

The most striking thing about this conclusion is the remarkable richness of meaning that gets attached to the idea of 'light', though the word itself appears only once. The advancing power of Dulness puts an end to the arts and sciences, man's means of expressing his superiority to the lower orders of creation, and the basic metaphor involves putting out various kinds of light. First 'fancy', the least valuable intellectual faculty to the Augustan way of thinking but nevertheless a useful one, is blotted out: 'Before her, *Fancy's* gilded clouds decay,/ And all her varying Rain-bows die away' (631–2). 'Gilded' suggests solidity of a sort, and 'decay' thus takes on a degree of metaphorical vitality. Though the clouds and rainbows consist of vapour, they do shine, transforming light into colour and pattern, and the hint of animation in 'varying' makes 'die', like 'decay', more than a dead metaphor. 'Wit' likewise is overcome: '*Wit* shoots in vain its momentary fires,/The meteor drops, and in a flash expires' (633–4). Wit, like fancy, is only momentary—its value is limited—but its destruction is also a blow to reasonable order. As a meteor it casts a temporary but brilliant light; yet with the advent of Dulness it expires 'in a flash', a last flare-up of light before permanent extinction.

But more important than fancy or wit, '*Art* after *Art* goes out, and all is Night'. At the approach of this 'dread Medusa' the very stars fade. Another mythological allusion focusses attention on the 'going out' of the Arts:

[6] Alwyn Berland, 'Some Techniques of Fiction in Poetry,' *Essays in Criticism*, IV, 1954, 379, argues, perhaps too ingeniously, that at the end of the *Dunciad* 'it is not the author who speaks, not any single character. . . . It is the *world* itself, the "character" about to be possessed by the fictional Dulness.'

> As Argus' eyes by Hermes' wand opprest,
> Clos'd one by one to everlasting rest;
> Thus at her felt approach, and secret might,
> *Art* after *Art* goes out, and all is Night (637-40).

Though there are many arts, they all relate to a single 'body'—civilization—which they inform and guide; the approach of the goddess is
'felt' and 'secret' not only because she is veiled in fog and gloom but
also because she heightens her invisibility by blinding her enemy, as
Hermes blinded Argus when rescuing Io. Truth flees to her original
cavern (the well from which Democritus claimed to have drawn her),
going out of light; philosophy, which by leaning on Heaven kept close
to the source of physical and spiritual light, now shrinks away to the
dim study of second causes; the other sciences gaze upon the approach-
ing darkness and go mad.

The end is utter blackness. 'Light dies before thy uncreating
word': the light of Genesis and the Word which St John says was in
the beginning are both obliterated by this new and blasphemous un-
Creation. Dulness can destroy the bases of order as God established
them and as man has kept them up, and the destruction of order equals
the destruction of reality as man knows it:

> Thy hand, great Anarch! lets the curtain fall;
> And Universal Darkness buries All.

The universal drama is over—the curtain shuts out the light, and
darkness buries not just literature and culture, but all creation.

The emphasis on light in this conclusion strongly suggests that
the image has more than local significance; and a seemingly-flat couplet may provide a bridge to the rest of the poem. When Dulness reigns
supreme:

> Nor *public* flame, nor *private*, dares to shine;
> Nor *human* Spark is left, nor Glimpse *divine*! (IV, 651-2).

The italics are Pope's, and the significant fact that these are the only
adjectives so emphasized in the poem seems to me to imply a hier-
archy of definitions which makes it possible to understand more fully
the function of 'light' in the whole poem.

The light of private intellectual activity, such fleeting illumination as
is cast by wit and fancy, does not stand very high in the Augustan
scale of values, as a glance at the opening lines of *Religio Laici* or *The
Hind and the Panther* will remind us. The extinction of 'public flame'
is more serious—the Augustans' deep concern for maintaining an
intelligible community of ideas and beliefs depends on the arts and the
links with tradition they provide. But Dulness goes even further:
the onslaught of darkness which obliterates every 'human spark',

public and private, also obscures the 'glimpse divine', the imperfect
but enriching vision of a higher light achieved through religious devotion. The uses of light and darkness in the body of the poem may
come into better focus if we bear this scale in mind. . . .

[Thomas R. Edwards then goes on to examine the imagery of light
and darkness in some detail].

The Fourth Book

[In the Fourth Book] the decay of literature mirrors the decay of
nature: verse loiters into prose just as order lapses into chaos, light
into darkness. Fame turns out to be doubly elusive—not only does the
poet die, but he finds little likelihood that his work will long survive
him. Both the poet and the song must yield to dullness, darkness,
and death.

A powerful vision of dissolution dominates the Fourth Book. . . .
The critical intelligence that made the poem possible must bow before
the irresistible onslaught of *nature*—a nature no longer seen as a
synonym for light and order but as a label for a ceaseless mutability
destroying all that makes life dignified or even possible.

This 'tragic' dimension of the *Dunciad* depends on the Fourth
Book and also upon the resonances which the more consistently
serious imaginative design of that Book strikes in what had been
written earlier. The 'sublimity' noted by Dr Leavis is concentrated
most thickly in the invocation to Book IV and the conclusion, and it
is such passages as these, when Pope uses Miltonic resources most
openly, that bring the underlying seriousness of the other books most
fully to life.[7] The poem in three books is more tidy as narrative than
the final version, just as the original *Rape of the Lock* is neater and
more 'exquisite' than the great poem Pope made from it; but without
the Fourth Book, and its open appeal for deep feeling and something
like the 'degree of horror' by which Burke was to identify the sublime,
it is hard to see how the *Dunciad* could have avoided at least a measure
of the oblivion that overtook its long-forgotten poetic offspring.[8]

It would of course be easy to overstate the case. The 'tragic' sublimity of the *Dunciad* does not overcome its positive, 'Augustan'
meaning, or at least not wholly. The threatened inevitable decay of
order, the triumph of entropy, never quite becomes a certainty. The

[7] F. R. Leavis, *Revaluation*, London, 1936, p. 90; *The Common Pursuit*,
p. 91. Samuel H. Monk, *The Sublime*, New York, 1935, p. 67, describes the
eighteenth-century vogue of the sublime as a movement away from the idea
that art reflects divine harmony and order.

[8] See Richmond P. Bond, 'IAD: a Progeny of the Dunciad,' *PMLA*, XLIV
1929, 1099–1105, for a discussion of eighteenth-century imitations of the poem.

tension between positive ideals and the recognition that reality poses
some disturbing challenges to those ideals does not snap, for even the
expressions of sublime terror and disgust remain within the bounds
of Pope's Augustan style. He can make beauty out of fright, just as
he can out of ugliness; the 'habits of thought and feeling' embodied
in the texture of his verse are sufficiently strong to control and direct
his vision of disorder. We may put it that in the *Dunciad* Pope's
'Augustanism' meets its sharpest challenge from the actual world and
triumphs—but the struggle, like Shakespeare's in the last plays, ex-
hausted the medium of expression, and Augustan sensibility was never
to triumph so finely again.

From 'Light and Nature: A Reading of the *Dunciad*', in *Philo-
logical Quarterly*, vol. XXXIX, no. 4, 1960, pp. 447–63.

GEORGE SHERBURN

The Dunciad, Book IV

... THROUGHOUT this part of *Dunciad* IV [lines 419–516] Pope is, of course, making an anti-rational appeal to common sense as an antidote to the metaphysics of rationalizing divines or deists. He opposes also all limited 'microscopic' technical study as well as the follies of travellers and elegant virtuosi. Both 'folly's cup' and 'wisdom's grave disguise' are scourged. Education fails because the pupil is made

> First slave to Words, then vassal to a Name,
> Then dupe to Party; child and man the same;
> Bounded by Nature, narrow'd still by Art,
> A trifling head, and a contracted heart.

What Pope commends is the humanly sympathetic and 'open' mind actuated by judgment and common sense: what he disapproves are metaphysics, the superficial follies of the wealthy, and the microscopic scholarship of men such as Bentley, Kuster, Burman, and Wasse. These scholars are mentioned by name, as are leading free-thinkers or theologians of the time. Concerning the virtuosi Pope is pseudonymously coy; but clearly his gallery of dunces is well filled and includes a rich assortment of all kinds. Poets and painters get off easily in this Book, and although Italian opera is ridiculed, we have in lines 65–70 the most famous and most timely compliment ever paid to Handel.[1]

So much for the intellectual content of the poem; its imaginative quality may be considered in two aspects—the structure of the Book as a whole and the specific quality of individual images.

The structural pattern of Book IV seems at first sight more original, less in the heroic tradition, than were the devices of the earlier Books.

---

[1] The great composer was, when Pope wrote these lines, bankrupt and in Ireland – producing among other things *Messiah*. He so appreciated Pope's praise that in his next opera (*Semele*, 1743) he inserted in Congreve's libretto the famous aria, 'Where'er you walk' – set to the words of Pope's *Summer*, lines 73–6.

Book I derived from *MacFlecknoe* and other sources; Book II, echoing
the funeral games for Anchises (*Aeneid* V), and Book III, drawing
from the prophetic visions of *Aeneid* VI and *Paradise Lost* XI and
XII, seem perhaps more normal for a mock epic. Book IV presents a
grand drawing-room, appropriate for a royal birthday, at which titles
or orders of merit are bestowed by the Queen of Dulness. The scene
is chiefly that of such a drawing-room, but it unfolds in a slightly con-
fusing dreamlike fashion into an academic meeting for the conferring
of degrees. This latter aspect of the scene intrigued both Pope and
Warburton, not merely because the *Dunciad* was a satire on pedantry,
but because in 1741 both Pope and Warburton had been proposed
for the LL.D. at Oxford, and since the grace was not voted for
Warburton, Pope declined it for himself. They were both unusually
'degree-conscious' at the time the poem was finished.

Book IV has been thought confused in structure; but there were
special reasons why its pattern of action was easily grasped in the
early 'forties. Henry Fielding in two or three very popular farces had
shown royal levees crammed with incongruous episodes that followed
each other kaleidoscopically much as do the passages of Book IV....

As models for his projected Book IV Fielding furnished Pope two
or three scenes from royal drawing-rooms. In the *Author's Farce*
(1730) he had scored with an uproarious scene from the drawing-room
of Queen Nonsense, and in 1736 *Pasquin* showed as rival queens
Common Sense and Ignorance, and the drawing-room of Queen
Ignorance was as confused and delightfully heterogeneous as a bear-
garden. In his *Historical Register* for 1736 an episode in Act III shows
'Apollo in a great chair, surrounded by attendants' and casting the
parts *à la* Cibber for Shakespeare's *King John*. Probably not Fielding's
(and certainly not Hesiod Cooke's) was a piece of similar structure,
called *The Battle of the Poets; or, The Contention for the Laurel*,
which was very briefly inserted in the second act of *Tom Thumb* just
before Cibber was made laureate. A scene with a foolish king or a mock
queen or goddess enthroned makes an admirable focal point about
which farcical episode may loosely revolve. These plays by Fielding
were enormously popular, and they almost certainly gave form to the
new Book of the *Dunciad*. Doubtless authors other than Fielding anticipated Pope in the use of this scene, but no other author at the time
had prepared Pope's public for the device as had Henry Fielding....

It is probable that Pope, who habitually composed in episodic frag-
ments, may have written parts of Book IV before he adopted the royal
drawing-room as a device for loose unification. We have his remark
to Spence about 'an Essay on Education; part of which I have inserted in the *Dunciad*,'[2] and at the point (line 138) where the inserted

[2] Spence, *Anecdotes*, ed. Singer, 1820, p. 315.

section begins, there is some wavering in the transitions. After the
stage is set, Opera in the first abrupt episode petitions for the silenc-
ing of Handel. There follows a curious passage (73–80) that states
Pope's strong and sincere concept of the positive attractive power of
Dulness for the many who instinctively swarm about the goddess
'conglob'd' like bees 'about their dusky Queen'. These 'naturally dull',
a footnote explains, are followed by the involuntarily dull, and by a
third group that are accidentally or temporarily dull. By the time we
reach line 101 the movement of these attendants has clarified and
become in some sort processional—

> There march'd the bard and blockhead, side by side.

And the stately stride of Montalto (Hanmer) is succeeded by the more
vigorous march of Bentley (lines 203 ff.), who in turn gives way to the
travelled fops (line 275). These successive groups, we are told in line
136, are

> Each eager to present the first Address.

But in the section on education that immediately follows no petitions
are presented. We have the early petition of Opera, and thereafter
none until the lac'd Governor naturally ends his presentation of his
foppish young traveller and the imported mistress (lines 282–335)
with a request for acceptance and protection. Annius follows at once
with a petition for aid in his numismatical 'cheating', and he is opposed
by Mummius. So likewise the petition of the expert in carnations is
opposed by the lover of butterflies. On the whole, one must conclude
the poet is preoccupied with description of the grotesque and mis-
cellaneous court rather than with a rehearsal of petitions: he seeks
diversity of episode fully as much as he does structural unity of the
whole. This tendency, in spite of all the learned have said, is quite
typical of English neo-classicism, and in this as in most of Pope's
poems episodes follow loosely in diverse and contrasting moods, just as
in a suite by Purcell or Handel an allegro is followed by an andante or
a courante by a rigadoon.

In all these contrasting episodes is apparent a rich variety in the
nature of individual images, a variety which is the immediate and chief
source of appeal in the poem. At the start of any consideration of these
it must be recognized that it is erroneous to think that Pope is deficient in concrete, highly specific imagery. His theory is not that of
'general effects secured through general details', though that may have
been the method of Sir Joshua Reynolds and other reputable
theorists. . . .

Himself a painter, Pope knew the value of a vivid phrase; he recognizes clearly the imaginative power of the highly specific, 'small' detail. It is true that in *Dunciad* IV many minute details do not now

come truly to life without the aid of annotation. Editors have done much, but the topical nature of satire still causes the casual reader perplexity. . . . Pope may be deficient in the conventional images of poetry—those drawn from nature or from such inspiring universals as love or death—but from first to last his satires are full of images that might occur to a modern realistic painter or poet. The French cook, 'a Priest succinct in amice white', would be merely a perfect 'Dutch piece' if Pope had not added the symbolism that elevates the gourmet's cult to a religious level, by means of the amice, the 'copious Sacrifice', and the dubious devotion due

> To three essential Partridges in one.

Pope recurs repeatedly to food-metaphors; a good example is lines 227–32 of Bentley's speech:

> For Attic Phrase in Plato let them seek,
> I poach in Suidas for unlicens'd Greek.
> In ancient Sense if any needs will deal,
> Be sure I give them Fragments, not a Meal;
> What Gellius or Stobaeus hash'd before,
> Or chew'd by blind old Scholiasts o'er and o'er.

These lines are typical of the vivifying use to which Pope can put metaphors in debasing intellectual matters that meet his contempt. Frequently his technical images are purely descriptive rather than (as in Bentley's speech) prejudicial. Take, for example, the intellectually apt couplet:

> Like buoys, that never sink into the flood,
> On Learning's surface we but lie and nod.

This is fair evidence of observation on the part of a poet whose sea-faring included only voyages on the Thames and one crossing to the Isle of Wight. We may be less content with his ingenuity in meaning when he writes

> See! still thy own, the heavy Canon roll,
> And Metaphysic smokes involved the Pole.

He may mean simply that the heavy artillery (of metaphysics) is always on the side of Dulness; but from his footnotes one must assume that he expects some Canon of Christ Church, Oxford, to feel that the smoke encircles a paranomasiac poll!

Less ingenious but more biting is such a picture as that of the complete exquisite, Paridel—

> Stretch'd on the rack of a too easy chair;

or the picture of the 'bowzy Sire', Thomas Gordon, less elegant in its
informality. He

> shook from out his Pipe the seeds of fire;
> Then snapt his box, and strok'd his belly down:
> Rosy and rev'rend, tho' without a Gown.
> Bland and familiar to the throne he came,
> Led up the Youth, and call'd the Goddess *Dame*.

In these somewhat 'homely' images Pope is at his best when dealing
with mankind; but he is not limited, and describes the crafty Annius
in rural terms:

> Soft, as the wily Fox is seen to creep,
> Where bask on sunny banks the simple sheep,
> Walk round and round, now prying here, now there;
> So he; but pious, whisper'd first his pray'r.

The poet brings to all this sort of thing a firm hand and an unerring
line—to borrow his own graphic phrase—but he does not altogether
limit himself to 'Dutch' realism. The grand tour of his fop leads to a
satiric gilding of the Italian lily that advertises the poet's skill in
metrics and in lush detail of artificial loveliness. The fop was guided

> To happy Convents, bosom'd deep in vines,
> Where slumber Abbots, purple as their wines:
> To Isles of fragrance, lily-silver'd vales,
> Diffusing languor in the panting gales:
> To bands of singing, or of dancing slaves,
> Love-whisp'ring woods, and lute-resounding waves.

Such imagery is pleasing but perhaps obvious. To see that Pope's
imagination is operating subtly throughout the poem one may wisely
consider the appropriate physical movements that vivify and charac-
terize the dull as they pass the throne of the goddess. Opera, the first,
is

> a Harlot form soft sliding by,
> With mincing step, small voice, and languid eye
>
>   .   .   .
>
> By singing Peers up-held on either hand,
> She tripp'd and laugh'd, too pretty much to stand.

Compare this with Sir Thomas Hanmer, the long-since Speaker of
the House of Commons, come to present to Dulness his edition of
Shakespeare:

> There mov'd Montalto with superior air;
> His stretch'd-out arm display'd a Volume fair;

> Courtiers and Patriots in two ranks divide,
> Thro' both he pass'd, and bow'd from side to side:
> But as in graceful act, with awful eye
> Compos'd he stood, bold Benson thrust him by:
> On two unequal crutches propt he came,
> Milton's on this, on that one Johnston's name.
> The decent Knight retir'd with sober rage,
> Withdrew his hand, and clos'd the pompous page.

After Sir Thomas

> crowds on crowds around the Goddess press,
> Each eager to present the first Address.

And among these were the university dons led by Richard Bentley:

> Before them march'd that awful Aristarch;
> Plow'd was his front with many a deep Remark:
> His Hat, which never vail'd to human pride,
> Walker with rev'rence took, and lay'd aside.
> Low bow'd the rest: He, kingly, did but nod;
> So upright Quakers please both Man and God.

After Bentley's address, not decently waiting its termination,

> In flow'd at once a gay embroider'd race,
> And titt'ring push'd the Pedants off the place. . . .

This marks a decline in vigorous movement, a decline that appropriately leads to the universal yawn. Paridel's relaxation is followed by the bowzy snoring of Silenus (Gordon): the diminuendo is now (line 493) marked, but throughout the Book the movement of the actors on Pope's stage is living and appropriate. He sees them move, and makes them visible to us.

Beauty is not the province of satire; and Pope's poem is not rich in pretty or alluring detail: realism, vigor, incisiveness are what we expect here—and find. . . .

Book IV of the *Dunciad* is so crammed with extremely diverse imagery that Joseph Warton, for example, thought it 'one of the most motley compositions, that, perhaps, is anywhere to be found in the works of so exact a writer as Pope'.[3]

But to leave the poem at that is a gross undervaluation both of Pope's organizing design—whether from Fielding or not—and, above all, of the basic integrity of his sense of intellectual values. Pope has a just prejudice against the dunce as an intellectual vacuum as well as

[3] Warton, *Essay on the Genius and Writings of Pope*, Fifth edition, 1806, II, 369.

against the dunce 'with loads of learned lumber in his head'. The fourth Book is not a contradiction of the first three Books: it is a richer and more imaginative restatement of the values announced in 1728 and 1729. . . .

From '*The Dunciad*, Book IV', in *Texas Studies in Literature and Language*, vol. XXIV, 1944, pp. 174–90.

SELECT BIBLIOGRAPHY

POEMS

Complete Editions

The Poems of Alexander Pope: The Twickenham Edition. General Editor, John Butt, 6 vols. in 7, London, 1939–61. This is the definitive edition.

The Poems of Alexander Pope, ed. John Butt, London, 1963, new ed. 1965. A one-volume edition of the Twickenham Text with selected annotations.

The Poetical Works of Alexander Pope, ed. Herbert Davis, London, 1966. Oxford Standard Authors Edition.

Selections

Useful selections are edited by P. Brockbank, London, 1964; D. Grant, London, 1965; R. P. C. Mutter and M. Kinkead-Weekes, London, 1962; W. K. Wimsatt, New York, 1951.

LETTERS

The Correspondence of Alexander Pope, ed. G. Sherburn, 5 vols. Oxford, 1956.

Letters of Alexander Pope, A selection edited by J. Butt, London, 1960.

BIOGRAPHY

George Sherburn, *The Early Career of Alexander Pope*, Oxford, 1934. The standard biography up to 1727.

Edith Sitwell, *Alexander Pope*, London, 1930. In spite of its sentimentality this book still has some value for its sympathetic account of Pope.

Joseph Spence, *Anecdotes, Observations, and Characters of Books and Men, Collected from the Conversation of Mr Pope and other Eminent Persons of His Time.*

(1) ed. S. W. Singer, 1820. Newly introduced by Bonamy Dobrée, London, 1964.

(2) ed. J. M. Osborn, 2 vols., Oxford, 1966. An essential source for Pope's life.

W. K. Wimsatt, *The Portraits of Alexander Pope*, New Haven and London, 1965. An interesting and beautifully produced book.

CRITICISM

Norman Ault, *New Light on Pope*, London, 1949.

Cleanth Brooks, 'The Case of Miss Arabella Fermor', in *Sewanee Review*, vol. LI, no. 4, 1943, pp. 505–24; also in *The Well Wrought Urn*, New York, 1947.

R. A. Brower, *Alexander Pope: The Poetry of Allusion*, Oxford, 1959. On the richness and meaning of classical allusion in Pope.

John Butt, *The Augustan Age*, London, 1950. Has a useful chapter on Pope.

J. S. Cunningham, *Pope: The 'Rape of the Lock'*, London, 1961. A detailed analysis of the poem.

T. R. Edwards, *This Dark Estate: A Reading of Pope*, Berkeley, 1963.

William Empson, 'Wit in the *Essay on Criticism*', in *The Hudson Review*, vol. II, no. 4, 1950, pp. 559–77; also in *The Structure of Complex Words*, London, 1951. Difficult but interesting.

Ian Jack, *Augustan Satire: Intention and Idiom in English Poetry 1660–1750*, Oxford, 1952. Chaps. V–VII.

Evan Jones, 'Verse, Prose and Pope: A Form of Sensibility', in *The Melbourne Critical Review*, No. 4, 1961, pp. 30–40.

Douglas Knight, *Pope and the Heroic Tradition, A Critical Study of His Iliad*, New Haven and London, 1951.

Arthur O. Lovejoy, *The Great Chain of Being*, Cambridge, Mass., 1936, repr. 1950. See Chaps. VI–IX for an illuminating study of some key ideas in the 18th century.

Maynard Mack, ed., *Essential Articles for the Study of Alexander Pope*, London, U.S.A. Printing, 1965. A valuable collection although of uneven quality. See in particular the essays by Auden, Brooks, Cameron, Empson, Griffith, Jack, Knight, Sutherland, Williams, and Wimsatt.

Maynard Mack, 'Wit and Poetry and Pope': Some Observations on his Imagery', in *Pope and his contemporaries: Essays presented to George Sherburn*, ed. J. L. Clifford and L. Landa, Oxford, 1949, pp. 20–40. The other essays in this book are also worth reading.

Rebecca Price Parkin, *The Poetic Workmanship of Alexander Pope*, Minneapolis, 1955.

M. Price, *To the Palace of Wisdom*, New York, 1964. Includes a good essay on Pope.

R. W. Rogers, *The Major Satires of Alexander Pope*, Urbana, Ill., 1955.

George Sherburn, 'Pope at Work', in *Essays on the Eighteenth Century Presented to David Nichol Smith*, Oxford, 1945, pp. 49–64.

J. Sutherland, *A Preface to Eighteenth Century Poetry*, London, 1948. A sound introduction to the period.

Geoffrey Tillotson, *On the Poetry of Pope*, London, 1938, rev. ed. 1950. The best book by a distinguished Pope scholar.

Geoffrey Tillotson, 'Alexander Pope, I and II', two essays in *Essays in Criticism and Research*, Cambridge, 1942.

A. L. Williams, *Pope's 'Dunciad': A Study of its Meaning*, London, 1955.

G. Wilson Knight, *The Poetry of Alexander Pope: Laureate of Peace*, London, 1955, Paperback 1965. See Chapter 'The Vital Flame', originally published in *The Burning Oracle*, London, 1939. The rest of the book is not as helpful as this chapter.

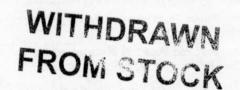